Pets Are Forever

*Every living thing on this planet
is connected at a base level.
Therefore we would create a better
and more certain future for ourselves and this world
by nurturing all the souls that dwell here.*

By the same author:

Past Life Angels

Souls Don't Lie

Past Life (meditation CD)

The Tree That Talked

How to Be Happy

Forever Faithful

Supernaturally True

Pets Have Souls Too

Angel Whispers

Soul Angels

Everyday Angels

Angels Please Hear Me

JENNY SMEDLEY

Pets Are Forever

Amazing True Stories of
Angelic Animals

HAY HOUSE

Australia • Canada • Hong Kong • India
South Africa • United Kingdom • United States

First published and distributed in the United Kingdom by:

Hay House UK Ltd, 292B Kensal Rd, London W10 5BE. Tel.: (44) 20 8962 1230;
Fax: (44) 20 8962 1239. www.hayhouse.co.uk

Published and distributed in the United States of America by:

Hay House, Inc., PO Box 5100, Carlsbad, CA 92018-5100. Tel.: (1) 760 431 7695
or (800) 654 5126; Fax: (1) 760 431 6948 or (800) 650 5115. www.hayhouse.com

Published and distributed in Australia by:

Hay House Australia Ltd, 18/36 Ralph St, Alexandria NSW 2015.
Tel.: (61) 2 9669 4299; Fax: (61) 2 9669 4144. www.hayhouse.com.au

Published and distributed in the Republic of South Africa by:

Hay House SA (Pty), Ltd, PO Box 990, Witkoppen 2068.
Tel./Fax: (27) 11 467 8904. www.hayhouse.co.za

Published and distributed in India by:

Hay House Publishers India, Muskaan Complex, Plot No.3, B-2, Vasant Kunj,
New Delhi – 110 070. Tel.: (91) 11 4176 1620; Fax: (91) 11 4176 1630.
www.hayhouse.co.in

Distributed in Canada by:

Raincoast, 9050 Shaughnessy St, Vancouver, BC V6P 6E5. Tel.: (1) 604 323 7100;
Fax: (1) 604 323 2600

© Jenny Smedley, 2011

A catalogue record for this book is available from the British Library.

ISBN 978-1-84850-290-1

Printed and bound in Great Britain by CPI Bookmarque, Croydon CR0 4TD.

Acknowledgements

This book is dedicated to all the horses, dogs, cats, chickens, ducks, rabbits and various wild birds and animals who have graced my life and taught me more than any human school could ever do.

My current dog, KC, has been very influential in collating this book.

My husband and best friend Tony has, as always, been my reliable sounding board.

Of course I also thank Hay House for their continuing trust in me.

I'd like to thank Bonnie Whitecloud, Co-ordinator of the Manataka American Indian Council, for getting permission for me to use the wise quotes of Grandfather Lee Standing Bear Moore in this book. It means a great deal to me.

Lastly, I'd like to thank Brian May, who is not only a musical legend in the eyes of the world, but a generous legend to me personally and to all the animals he gives his time to help.

The soul is the same in all living creatures, although the body of each is different.

– HIPPOCRATES

Some say knowledge of the natural power of animal guides has been lost. This is not so. Many people think animals are not spiritual – having no spirit or soul. Most think animals are less intelligent than humans, savage and without society or conscience.

This is not so.

– GRANDFATHER LEE STANDING BEAR MOORE
(THROUGH HIS FRIEND TAKATOKA)

Contents

Foreword – Dr Brian H May CBE   xiii

Preface   xvii

Introduction   xxiii

Chapter 1   You Stupid Dog!   **1**
*Do humans have the right to call animals
stupid? Are animals as spiritual, or even
more spiritual than we are? Stories of
animals who have helped those of other
species*

Chapter 2   Forever Faithful   **15**
*Pets who return to visit their owners after
death*

Chapter 3   Guardians Who Never Leave Us   **33**
*Pets who have reappeared after death to
protect their owners*

Chapter 4 **I'm Back!** **57**

Pets who have regenerated and come back to their owners in a new body, sometimes even in the body of a different species

Chapter 5 **Animal Angels** **73**

Pets who have been infused with the spark of an angel, sometimes for a moment and sometimes for a whole lifetime

Chapter 6 **Magical Healers** **91**

Pets who have healed their owners or helped their owners heal other people

Chapter 7 **Mystical Pets** **121**

Animals who can see and communicate with spirits. Telepathic pets

Chapter 8 **Wild Animals** **137**

Is the fox a cold-blooded killer? Does the lion feel sorry for its prey? Are animals innocent?

Chapter 9 **Abuse of Animals** **143**

Is it wrong to perceive animals as here merely for human consumption and sport? Does intensively farming animals harm the soul of the person who does it?

Chapter 10   Time Travel with Your Pet   151

How to rewrite your pets' scripts to heal
their illnesses and apparent behaviour
problems that have been generated by
past-life energy and current life trauma

Chapter 11   Starting Out Right   163

If you're unsure of where to look for your
compatible pet soulmate, numerology and
other modalities can help you make the
best start

Chapter 12   Expert Help   179

Advice on where to go for help if you're
unable to make your own connection with
your pet

Afterword   217

Recommended Reading   219

Resources   221

Foreword

Jenny Smedley is already a name known to animal lovers worldwide, but for those to whom her name is new, let me explain a little. Her thesis — that animals have souls as well as humans — can easily be mistaken for a piece of pure 'sentimentality'. But the lightness and humour of many of the anecdotes in this book belie a subtext which is the power behind a very important and growing revolution in our attitude to the other species on Planet Earth. In my work for Animal Welfare in recent months, I have been struck by a very clear insight. We all grow up, and leave home, and are sure that our system of beliefs is entirely our own, supported by verifiable evidence and logical argument. But for the vast majority of us, nothing could be further from the truth. We don't have to look very far into our everyday behaviour to see that it is dominated by habit

– a whole system of behaviour patterns learned from our parents or guardians in our early childhood, only marginally modified by ourselves, often in response to pressure from our peers in later life.

These behaviours are based on mainly unquestioned beliefs, and many of them relate to the way we treat animals. Many of us eat the flesh of animals daily, reassured by the echoes of our parents' voices in our heads: 'You need your protein' … 'It's good for you', etc. In spite of mountains of clear evidence that a vegetarian diet is much healthier for our bodies, much more beneficial to the health of our planet and, if adopted by all, would vastly decrease the suffering of animals, these old beliefs, and these behaviours, persist. Ah – the *suffering* of animals? Here is where we are liable to be accused of sentimentality, of anthropomorphism. Many of us in our youth were given open or implied messages such as, 'Animals don't suffer in the same way we do,' or 'Animals are there for us to use any way we want,' or 'Animals are dirty,' or 'Some animals are vicious, some are pests, vermin – must be *controlled*,' or 'It's brave to kill animals.' So daily, millions upon millions of farm animals are cruelly abused, millions of animals are used in horrific experiments in the name of making humans live longer, or look prettier, and what is left of our wild animals have no rights – can be stalked, trapped, snared, shot, or torn apart by men with packs of dogs. Even a quick look at all this by a visiting alien would lead him to the conclusion that the human race, while rather laughably considering itself to be more or less the only important species on the planet, comes out as the most badly behaved. The alien would conclude that our behaviours are mainly governed by instinct and that, while we are anatomically almost indistinguishable from the other mammals on Earth, we refuse to admit their similarity to us, and refuse to recognize their right to live and breathe in peace. Jonathan Safran Foer, in his book *Eating Animals*, alerted me to a word I had not encountered before: anthropodenial – the illogical denial of the fact that the animals around us see, hear and feel almost exactly as we do; they also feel pleasure, pain and fear, and it is the denial of these truths which licenses those lacking in empathy to try to justify the cruelty they inflict, or assent to.

All this might seem a long way away from a book which is full of lightness and joy, and insights into animal thinking, emotion and abstract thought. But as you dip into these stories, you will find constant triggers ... reminders that we need to constantly question the edicts of old ways of thinking. At my Sunday School, at the age of about ten, we were taught that '*Only humans have souls – only humans can go to Heaven.*' It bothered me for years – it seemed grossly unfair, and I fiercely resisted the notion that my cat might be turned away from the Gates of Heaven. The thought often returns to me even now. Of course there is no evidence for that teaching at all, and it must have justified countless unnecessary acts of cruelty and neglect of animals through the ages. On every page of this book, I am reassured that it's just another old belief which needs to be thrown out of the window, for lack of evidence. No! More than that – thrown out owing to clear evidence to the contrary, recounted with great skill and dedication in this book.

You can be sure of it. As Ms Smedley says … *Animals have souls, too!*

Brian May
2010

Preface

All my life I've been obsessed with animals, and I've often been fonder of them than of most people that I've known. There was never a point at which I wondered if they had souls like us, because I'd always known they had. Since writing *Pets Have Souls Too*, and now this book, I've seen enough evidence that they do have souls to be able to convince any reasonable person to agree with me.

People sometimes say that there's no mention of animals having souls, or going to Heaven, in the Bible. But that isn't surprising and doesn't mean they don't. After all, the Bible is said to be an instruction manual for humans to follow in order for them to achieve the grace to be permitted into Heaven, but animals can't read, so why would there be any instructions about them in the human instruction manual? If you still doubt, then try to imagine a Heaven that has no animals in it. It's impossible. But in any case, there are Bible quotes that really do seem to indicate the importance and spiritual value of animals, and these messages are, clearly, meant for us humans.

WORDS ABOUT ANIMALS, HEAVEN AND SPIRITUALITY

The same fate awaits man and animals alike.

– GENESIS 9:13-17

Then I saw Heaven opened, and behold, a white horse.

– REVELATIONS 19:11

The lesser creatures await Christ's return to redeem the sons of God so they, too, will be released from physical death to eternal life.

– ROMANS 8:19

Do animals exist forever? Do they have an immortal soul like us? The real question to ask is: what qualifies living beings to be admitted into Heaven after they die? The simple answer to me is that they must have a soul, and to make this a reality they have to have shown the ability to love and to feel compassion.

On 4 December 2008, a story was captured on a motorway camera in Santiago, in Chile. At first sight the film looked like it was going to be just another tragic road victim tale, as a dog ran across the carriageways. Appearing to be in a blind panic, the dog paid no attention to the continuous speeding traffic, and the inevitable soon happened: the poor dog was struck a glancing blow by two cars and was left, sprawled unconscious and obviously badly injured or dead, right in the middle of the carriageway. It looked as if this dog was soon to be reduced to a smear on the tarmac, but then on the edge of the camera's range another dog appears. This second dog pauses for a moment, as if assessing the problem, and then carefully makes his way across the lanes of traffic to the prone dog. He shows huge understanding as he waits for and negotiates brief gaps in the traffic. At this point, for me, the images become quite surreal, as the rescuer dog doesn't grasp the injured one with his mouth, the way you might expect a dog to, but instead stands behind his companion's head and puts a front leg either side, with his paws under the injured dog's armpits. Then, step by painstaking step, the dog walks backwards across the motorway, dragging his friend, looking carefully at the traffic each time he crosses a lane, still able to avoid the speeding cars, until he reaches the safety of the grass.

Sadly, this miracle didn't have a really happy ending, as the first dog had apparently died on impact, and his rescuer ran away before the motorway workers, who came running to the scene to help, could take it to be re-homed. But there are many things to consider in this story. How was the second dog able to assess the situation so intelligently? If he was just a 'dumb animal', how did he know that his friend needed rescuing? If he was incapable of love, then why would he care anyway? The dog was obviously very clever to be able to make it unscathed onto, across and off the three-lane road, but when he reached the other dog, he must have been able to sense that it was too late to save his life, and yet something drove him to still want his friend's body off the road. Why would a dog care what happened to a dead body and pull it so laboriously off the road, instead of just saving himself? Did he want his friend's body to be respected? If so, this is hardly the thought process of an irrational mind. Why did he use the totally human way of dragging the other dog, instead of grasping him with his teeth, which would have made his journey back much safer and quicker? Over and above all these remarkable questions, the biggest one of all remains: why did the dog embark on the rescue in the first place? There can be only one answer. He loved the other dog.

There was a story featured in the UK national press recently about an orphaned orang-utan (orphaned by humans) that had been brought to a rescue centre in a zoo. It was grief-stricken, because animals do feel grief, just as we do. She wouldn't eat and it looked to her carers as if she were going to give up and die. At the same time a sick dog was found nearby, abandoned. The two animals bonded instantly. It didn't matter that they were of different species. Perhaps they recognized similar emotions in each other. The fact is that this unlikely pair became inseparable.

There were two feral cats recently featured on the internet. One had been hit by a car and lay dead in the gutter. The cat's companion astonished onlookers by standing on top of his dead friend and appearing to administer CPR, massaging the other cat's abdomen with his paws as if trying to make it breathe again. The cat did this for two hours before he would let anyone remove the dead body.

Some other easily observed characteristics which I believe demonstrate animals' right to be admitted to Heaven are the following:

- **Animals are not judgmental about others, and they don't prejudge others based on their personal appearance. They are not prejudiced against anyone of any race or sexual orientation or religious belief system.**

- Animals don't care whether their companions are the same colour or a different colour to themselves. A black dog is treated exactly the same as a white dog, and of course this is only common sense because under their fur and skin they are exactly the same.

Human language has brought many benefits, but on the other hand it has moved us away from natural communication, by body language, which is of course the method of connection on which animals rely. We could truly learn a lot from our animal friends, not least of which would be to ask ourselves a little more often the question, 'Who are we to say who does and does not deserve a heavenly afterlife?' I feel it's my duty to ask this question, and that's why I have written this book.

Introduction

My dog KC told me recently, 'We are the same as you. We're just like people,' and this is the message of this book. Animals are just like us in the way they feel and in the fact that they are immortal.

Anyone who owns a pet of any kind and loves it knows the terrible trauma that accompanies losing a pet. It is, indeed, just as bad as losing a person. It's no surprise, though, because pets give us a type of unconditional love that's unmatched in the world. In fact, even an animal that's been abused by its owner all its life will often still look upon that person with love and devotion.

KC has been with me through many lives in many different bodies. The most recent one before this was when her soul was encased in the body of Ace, my German Shepherd cross Labrador. Ace was a big black dog, and anyone who met her during her prime couldn't fail to be either impressed by her beauty or intimidated by her power, and which one of the two they perceived depended on their intentions. She was normally the gentlest creature, even cleaning and nurturing any of our newborn lambs that were rejected by their mothers, but let anyone threaten to lay a hand on me or the rest of her 'pack' and she would change instantly into a tiger.

This image of her is a far cry from when she came to us. At that point she'd been a 13-week-old pathetic, scarred little bundle of insecurity. Her previous owner had burned her, leaving her chest and the top of one leg mostly hairless. At the time the rescue centre that had saved her were having trouble re-homing her. People didn't relish the thought of walking down the street with a scarred dog on a lead, worried perhaps that passersby might think they were the ones that had inflicted the damage on her. Other people had tried to home her but found her too clingy, too desperate, too scared and basically too much trouble. None of these things worried us. From the moment when this traumatized puppy walked the few paces from the rescue lady and sat quietly at my side, as if to say, 'Thank goodness, you've come at last,' she owned us, mind, body and soul.

There followed a few years when alternately she saved me from an enraged ram and an intruder, and I saved her from a rampaging swarm of wasps and a near-drowning in the local river. We came to trust one another implicitly. I worried, almost from the start, and increasingly over the years, how I'd ever cope with losing her. It's a cruel trick, having dogs not live as long as their masters. Of course when it did eventually happen, as it inevitably had to, and Ace lay lifeless on our living room floor, I simply couldn't cope with the bottomless chasm her absence created in my heart. For six months I grieved constantly, crying at some point every day, sobbing when my hand reached for what had been her constant presence, only to find empty space. No more, I vowed. I would never have another dog. For one thing, I didn't want any other dog that wasn't her. And I knew that I couldn't stand another loss like that one. It was better, I thought, not to love and lose.

I was wrong. We can never have too much love in our world, despite the pain it can bring.

Tony and I went to Arizona, to the beautiful and mystical town of Sedona for our first holiday in years. There I had a psychic reading during which the medium, unasked, tapped into 'a big black dog with grey whiskers'. I was told that this dog was 'a spark of my soul', and with this information came a sort of epiphany. I came to understand one of the great truths. When pets are so connected that the relationship between them and their owner almost transcends that of two humans, and when the understanding between the two is so remarkable that it verges on telepathic, then those pets are sparks, part of their owner's soul. The comfort in this, and what I felt instantly, is that these two can never really be parted.

Some people have spoken to me of a feeling of being hit in the chest some time after their pet has passed, and that the gentle blow lifts them out of their spiralling depression following the loss of their companion. This 'blow' is the feeling they get when the spark of their soul, the one that resided in their pet, comes back to them. It's a reunion on a spiritual level and completes the person once again. No wonder the pain of one of these pets passing is so dire and deep. No wonder a person in that position feels as if part of them is missing, for it is exactly that.

The medium also told me that Ace said, 'Today I'm young again.' We didn't quite understand the true significance of this until we were back home and had our attention drawn to a litter of 'Springadors' (Springer Spaniels cross Labradors) which had been born on the very same day that I'd had the reading in Arizona. When we went to see them, as we had to, a feeling a déjà vu stole over us as this strangely quiet puppy behaved toward me in exactly the same way as Ace had when we'd first met her. When the puppy turned over in my arms and displayed her pink tummy, we could see that she had been born with a nipple missing – the same nipple Ace had lost in surgery a few years before she'd died. That wasn't the end of the story, either. A few weeks later I received a drawing from psychic artist June-Elleni Laine, which she said had come to her from a black German Shepherd cross Labrador, with the message, 'This is me.' The drawing was an exact portrayal, in every detail, of the new puppy that we'd called KC. Ace had returned to us in a new body.

AMAZING DOG CONVERSATION

Recently we had a visit from animal communicator Jackie Weaver. She was collecting material for her new book, *Celebrity Pet Talking*, and wanted to do a reading with KC to put in it. It was a remarkable experience. I am of course able to communicate with KC on a day-to-day basis, but sometimes, as with all readings of a psychic nature, if you're too close to the subject, it's hard to know exactly how much your personal knowledge impinges on what you feel when it comes to the important questions. In Jackie's case she had no knowledge at all of KC, so everything was clear and simple and not to be misunderstood or over-interpreted. To me, the fact that people can communicate with animals adds weight to the evidence of them having souls. When Jackie came along and proved conclusively that she could indeed 'talk' to KC, it was great confirmation of what I already knew. Jackie was able to describe KC's favourite walk, the exact terms of endearment I use on a daily basis, and pinpoint precisely the seat of KC's previous lameness – though all of these things could, to the sceptic, be extremely good guesses. So when Jackie came up with the next item I was very pleased because I defy anyone to doubt it. She asked KC if I ever did anything that had impressed her, and if there were anything I did that she thought I was good at. KC 'told' her in thought that she'd been quite impressed watching me take a lot of trouble drawing some specific shapes and details on something she described as two circles that looked a bit like a piece of machinery, all the while accompanied by a quiet 'buzzy' noise. What Jackie did not know, could not possibly know, is that the day before I'd spent a couple of hours on the computer designing a CD cover for my good friend Madeleine Walker (Jackie does not know her, either). The design was based around a double circle, with various intricate, symmetrical shapes such as hearts, stars and moons around it and in it. It did take a lot of time and effort as it was the first time I'd attempted such a thing. KC had sat and watched the whole time, and listened to the constant 'buzz' of my computer's whirring brain. To me this message was indisputable proof that Jackie was able to communicate with my dog.

BUNNY HUGGER?

Some sceptics will probably label me a 'bunny hugger' – all emotion and no realism. This isn't true. While I love all animals, I also respect them and their place in the scheme of things.

Of recent times there's been a lot of press about foxes. Some people see them as part of Nature and appreciate their beauty. Others see them as a threat, either to their livelihood or even their person. Some people want to protect them, others to eradicate them mercilessly. Some of these are the people with all emotion and no sense. To kill another creature is sometimes necessary, but to enjoy that killing and treat it as sport is not. I accept all parts and all the aspects of the fox's nature, as I can demonstrate in the following two tales.

THE BRAVEST DUCK

We used to keep ducks for a while for their eggs, and occasionally we'd have a visit from a fox. One day we failed to see a hole in the netting before we went out and were gone for several hours. The fox got in and, yes, it killed or attacked every bird. For fun? No. It was for survival.

We took the blame for the birds' deaths because, the way I see it quite honestly, we had built a 'fast food restaurant' in the middle of the foxes' territory (by setting up a chicken coop) so we couldn't really blame the foxes for wanting to sample the fare. I always felt it was up to us to keep the birds safe. We were very upset naturally to see the coop empty of life and with the dead birds laid out in a line next to the hole in the fence. But the birds were dead, so we left them and the fox came back repeatedly and collected the birds one at a time, taking them off to stock its larder. The only reason foxes appear to kill everything and then abandon the bodies, giving rise to the belief that they kill for fun, is because they've been disturbed. Left alone, they won't waste a single death.

I say the fox killed them all, but we did find one duck alive. She'd been bitten through the neck, though, and although the vet was able to save her life, he couldn't do anything about the nerve damage she'd sustained. We thought about having her humanely destroyed, but after watching her for a while we couldn't bring ourselves to have this done. You see, that duck showed more courage and determination than any animal I'd ever seen. She would try to walk and the nerve damage in her neck would cause her to tumble over backwards. Undaunted, she'd get to her feet and try again, and again, never ever giving up. How could we not give her a chance? Miraculously she gradually became able to keep her balance for longer and longer, and a few weeks later she had just a slight twist in her neck to show for her ordeal. She taught me a lot about persistence and perseverance, and I never hated the fox, for it had no cruel intent.

SAVING MR FOX

When we moved home in Somerset a few years ago, we made sure we weren't smack bang in the middle of a hunt's territory. All around us was land where hunting wasn't allowed, either with gun or dog. We weren't going to witness any atrocities, or so I thought.

One Tuesday afternoon I was sitting in the conservatory thinking how funny it was that all the pheasants in the area seemed to congregate in our garden. My hubby, Tony, always reckoned I called them in. We could hear guns, but only off in the far distance, and the birds would have been perfectly safe anywhere in the village. But every day they came, dozens of them, male and female. Tony said that they were attracted by my thought waves, knowing they'd be safe near me. Maybe he was right because it wasn't long before a peacock in full regalia also turned up and then, incredibly, a pair of moorhens, even though we had no water in the garden!

Anyway, back to that Tuesday. In the distance I could hear a strange sound, and we suspected after a while that it was a hunting horn. We couldn't see any horses or riders, though, and we're quite high up so we figured they were miles away. The huntsmen might have been, but it turned out their hounds weren't. Hunts nowadays follow trails, as hunting has, quite rightly, been banned, but hounds don't always follow the right scent and can stray onto a 'live' one. They are notoriously hard to control once they hit a scent, and hunts can't always get them back on track. This is why I feel the law needs to be tightened up.

The first sign that there'd be trouble came when I heard the distinct telepathic voice of a fox in severe distress. It was literally screaming out in terror. I stood up.

'What?' asked Tony.

'It's a fox – they've got a fox…' I answered. 'Come on!' I dashed outside, followed by Tony. We couldn't see anything. Then we heard hounds, baying, coming closer.

I cried out to the fox in my mind, 'Come here boy, come on.' I could sense it was a male, a big dog fox. 'He's coming!' I yelled, legging it down our garden, which spanned about an acre. Tony followed.

Within a minute the fox popped out of the hedgerow and stood, panting, in front of us. I looked over the far side to a thick shrub. The fox got the message and ran that way, climbing up into the shrub.

Within another minute about 20 hounds poured into the garden. Heads down, oblivious to us, they started to track across the garden toward the shrub. Hounds are big dogs, and 20 is a lot of dogs of any size. I planted myself between them and the fox. There was no way we could really physically stop them. There were too many and so focused on their prey that whatever we'd done they would have taken no notice of us.

There was only one thing for it. At any second they'd find the fox and tear him to bits. I closed my eyes and thought myself into the hounds' minds. I pictured them going back the way they'd come. My mind ached with the pressure of it, and then I suddenly felt a switch in their collective pack mind and opened my eyes. They were streaming away, back through the hedge and into the adjacent land. We weren't out of the woods yet, though. I had to keep concentrating, removing the scent of fox from our hedge. This went on for about 40 minutes, the hounds milling around next door, mystified as to where their quarry had gone.

Finally, just when I was getting exhausted, we heard the sound of a rapidly trotting horse going up the road. It was obviously a huntsman searching for his hounds because he was blowing his horn like mad. The hounds finally broke off their search and obeyed the call. It was ten minutes before Mr Fox was brave enough to leave his cover and slink away. He spared us a glance of thanks as he went on his way.

SECRET WORLD FOX

During my time at Taunton TV as a presenter, one of my greatest pleasures was when we filmed live at the Secret World Wildlife Rescue Centre. One visit involved me being inside the fox enclosure. There were about six foxes in there: some that had been handed over by misguided people who had tried to keep them as pets, and some that had been found injured and nursed back to health but were not fit enough to be returned to the wild. Within minutes of my sitting down in the enclosure, the foxes had swarmed over me, and one female spent many minutes scenting on me by rubbing her head over mine. I was told by the keeper that this meant she was making me a part of her family. I was incredibly honoured to be accepted in this way, and a video clip of the event can be seen on my website. During my filming with Secret World I also experienced a barn owl sitting on my shoulder, a bat squirming around in the warmth inside my sweater and being literally covered from head to foot in ferrets!

THE PONY WITH HOMING INSTINCT

When I was young I longed to own my own pony, but it wasn't to happen until I was in my twenties. However, children and animals have a special bond if they love each other, and I wasn't short on opportunities to learn this.

My dad knew a man who lived about ten miles from us. He was a rough diamond, someone who dealt in scrap metal, and he always had a pony or two around the place. He let me ride a little pony of his called Jigsaw. He was very pretty, a blue roan, quite small but very strong and effervescent. I loved him, and we certainly bonded, but I'd only been going to ride him for a couple of weeks when his owner rang with some sad news: Jigsaw had broken out of his paddock and vanished. It was very odd that a pony would run away from his secure home, but it seemed as if he had. I persuaded my dad to drive me around in the car near to where Jigsaw lived in the hopes that we'd come across him, but we didn't. The police were informed but nobody came forward to say they'd found him. It was a mystery. A few days later I was out walking and passed by a yard behind a café, about half a mile from where I lived. Through the open gateway I could see two men trying to corner a pony. I couldn't believe my eyes: it was Jigsaw! The men saw me looking and called out to ask if I knew of anyone who'd lost a pony. Even they couldn't believe it when I told them the pony had come from the town ten miles away. To get to this place he'd had to cross two major 'A' roads and make his way through acres of woodland and farms. The fact that he'd ended up in my backyard, so to speak, and without anyone seeing him, was really odd. Although he'd been acting wild with the men who were trying to catch him, he calmed immediately as I walked up to him and tamely allowed me to put a halter on him. Why did he run away? How did he end up there? Had he been trying to find me? I really think he had.

ASHLEY PEACOCK

When the peacock arrived in our garden out of the blue one day, we were suitably impressed, but just with his beauty. It wasn't until quite recently, when someone remarked on how strange it was, that we realized there was more going on than meets the eye. This same person, Jo Phillips, a BBC journalist, remarked during her visit that it was refreshing to find a 'spiritual' author who actually made sure that something new was included in every book. She went on to say that some authors seem to write the same book over and over again. I was very gratified to hear her opinion of my work. Later she emailed me to say that she'd looked up what peacocks represent:

The peacock represents some of the most admired human characteristics and those that most of us would aspire to. An accepted symbol of integrity, its beauty shows us what we too can achieve when we have the courage to stick to our guns and show our true colours. In other cultures the peacock symbolizes nobility, honour, guidance, protection and alertness.

Jo Phillips very kindly said that this animal symbol was very appropriate to us and our home.

This conversation was important and reminded me of some vital messages. As I said, this peacock just turned up in the garden one day. He gradually became tamer as he got to know both us and KC, who understood very quickly that he wasn't considered an intruder and shouldn't be harassed by her. We soon named him 'Ashley', after Ashley Peacock in *Coronation Street*, and he must have approved because he readily answers to that name. While he spends a lot of time in our garden, he is also a free spirit, able to leave at any time, and this was an important part of the message he was bringing. I write regularly for magazines and my columns bring with them a certain amount of pressure (timescales and deadlines) as well as great responsibility. I've often noticed that psychics of all kinds who appear on

TV are under extraordinary pressure to perform, and having worked in live TV for two years myself I understand the timescales and commercialism of the media. It must be difficult to force things sometimes, to perform 'to order', for time is money on TV. I feel this peacock is a reminder to me that I must maintain my integrity at all times, and that any modest abilities I may have could vanish just as quickly as they seemed to arrive. Like the legend of the ravens at the Tower of London, should the peacock ever desert me I would know that my downfall would have been of my own making. I have been warned!

I had to add something to this chapter today. We're having some building work done and, as is usual when there's any disturbance going on at the house, Ashley had disappeared off elsewhere. The problem was that a week later we still hadn't seen or heard from him. Usually even if he's not in our garden we can hear him 'hooting' in the distance, but not this time. As he is a free spirit we have no say over where he chooses to be, whether he gets across the road safely or whether a predator, animal or human, might harm him, so we got increasingly worried as the days went by and there was no sign. Then I woke up at 4 a.m. because I was so concerned, and I lay there brooding over his possible fate and how to discover it. We'd already driven up and down the lane to make sure he wasn't lying injured on the road somewhere, but, like anyone when the 'night nadgers' strike, I became very down about it. Then I thought, *so talk to him!* And I started to call to him in my mind, asking him to please give us a sign that he was all right – or, indeed, a sign if he was not. My restlessness woke Tony up, too, and at 5 a.m. he got up, only to immediately call back to me from the kitchen, 'Ashley's out on the patio!' I was so relieved! He stayed with us all day, carefully watching the building progress and examining the workers' lunch at midday, and then he glided away, his long tail sweeping the ground like a bride's train. This time I won't worry if he doesn't come back while the work's going on because I know that he can 'hear' me.

My belief is that animals are just as important as we are in the wide-angle view of things. When we eradicate a species, through design or accident, we have no way of knowing what long-term effect this might have on us. Our planet, our eco-system and our way of life are very fragile. We upset the balance at our peril. We rely heavily on some of the smallest of God's creatures for our very survival. Take bees, for instance. Without their pollinating skills the keystone would soon fall out of humanity's wall, and yet their decline is being treated like something fairly trivial. I am also extremely saddened and upset by the growing number of our children committing violent crimes against others. I truly feel that if children were all brought up to respect and care for animals, they would grow up into decent adults who cared for others. I think all children should have pets, but, vitally, they should be taught to look after them and to understand that all living things feel pain and sorrow. Animals can teach humans a lot about spirituality.

Ask the animals, and they will teach you.

– JOB 12:7-10

CHAPTER 1

You Stupid Dog!

Do humans have the right to call animals stupid? Are animals as spiritual, or even more spiritual than we are? Stories of animals who have helped those of other species

Man has long attempted to re-establish communication with animals while trying to teach apes, dolphins and other animal species sign language and human sounds of speech. Why? Why do they try to make them walk up a mountain backwards? Animals do not possess the physical or mental ability for human speech, so why do they try? If humans are so intelligent, would it not make more sense for humans to learn animal speech?

– GRANDFEATHER LEE STANDING BEAR MOORE
(THROUGH HIS FRIEND TAKATOKA)

WHO'S THE STUPID ONE?

It's sadly common to hear people who are struggling with their pets' behaviours to call them stupid. Cries of, 'You stupid dog/cat/horse!' or whatever can be heard everywhere. The problem is that people treat their pets as if they understand human speech, human priorities and human desires. They're not human in character or ability, but that certainly doesn't make them stupid! A horse is a very clever horse, a dog is a very clever dog, a cat is a very clever cat, etc. There's no doubt that humans are very clever … for humans, that is. It would be no good animals having the brainpower to work a computer, for instance, as they have no desire or need to. On the other hand, try leaving a man stranded in the desert and tell him to smell his way to the water, and we'd soon see that he'd make a very stupid animal indeed! Animals haven't lost their God-given sense of smell as we have, and they can easily find water by the characteristic smell of the soil and the micro-organisms with which it mixes. Can the animal tell you the chemical formula of this smell like a human chemist could? No. But could the chemist smell what she can name in a vast area of wilderness? No.

So which of these is clever and which is stupid? The answer is neither one. They're both clever in their own way! It would make for a better world if we accepted and valued the differences between species, instead of making comparisons.

Using tools is recognized as a sign of great reasoning. Many, many animals use tools. Everyone knows that monkeys use tools, such as rocks to break shells and sticks to pick termites out of holes, but dolphins too have learned to put a piece of sea sponge on their noses to protect them from being scraped by the seabed when they're searching along it for food. This has been happening for some years and so is learned behaviour, which is another sign of great intelligence.

Recently, the University of Vienna carried out some experiments in abstract conceptualizing with dogs. Previously this was a skill thought only to exist in primates. Two dogs were shown a touch screen and soon learned that if they chose the image of a dog rather than that of a landscape, they'd get a reward. They scored consistently well and, further, even when they were shown the dog image superimposed over the image of the landscape, they were able to pick out the dog by pushing at it with their noses.

Chimps have been recognized as being very intelligent, but in Kyoto, in Japan, new experiments have revealed that they could actually beat human competitors when it comes to short-term memory. They did this by remembering a sequence of numbers which was only displayed to them for one second, something the human guinea pigs couldn't match.

Parrots are very clever by any standards. They can sort things by colour and not only repeat the names of objects, but do so correctly, identifying them in a way that shows cognitive intelligence. They can also solve puzzles, thus demonstrating an ability to follow cause and effect. Some parrots have even learned to string conceptual sentences together.

Birds in general often display great cleverness. Our village peacock fascinates me every evening. He always spends the hours before darkness in our garden, but actually leaves just before dark to sleep in a garden across the road. He clambers over our roof first, clomping away as if wearing hobnailed boots, and then he flies down into the front garden. He pauses at the gate and cocks his head from side to side, listening intently. Often we can hear nothing, but if he doesn't move off down the road, you can be absolutely sure that in seconds a car will approach, or some unheard (by us) cyclists or pedestrians. Once the coast is clear, off he goes, over the road to bed. On the first day of our recent building work he seemed to patrol the grounds around the house and inspected every area of work that was going on. He even came inside one room after the existing door was removed to see what was going on in there.

RODENT OR RESCUER?

Many people shudder at the mention of a rat. Some don't like their naked tails, or their scratchy claws or 'beady' eyes. I've never felt that way. This poor creature has also been reviled for plague-carrying, when it's actually their fleas that transmitted the plague diseases. I understand that numbers in the wild have to be kept in check because they do have the capacity to pass on some diseases in their urine if they are infected and live in too close a proximity to us, but would insist that control is done humanely. I'm sure there must be a way that the wild rat population could be fed with a drug concealed in food that would curtail their admittedly unequalled breeding abilities!

Tame rats can make wonderful pets. They are intelligent, affectionate and disease-free if kept correctly. In any case, nowadays some ratty populations have redeemed themselves in the eyes of many by being extremely instrumental in saving human lives, and I don't mean in abhorrent laboratory experiments!

These are the giant rats of Mozambique. The size of a large cat, these rats have been trained to sniff out the lethal explosives hidden under the ground in landmines, left over from one of mankind's many battles against his own kind. These rats are going to be used in other countries which have these dangerous leftovers, too. Known by their trainers as smart, sociable and sensitive, the rats are loved by them. The giant rats' noses are far more sensitive than all current mechanical vapour-detectors, and they can detect the faintest whiff of TNT or other explosives. Because the animals are lightweight compared to humans, they don't trigger the explosives, which when located can then be safely defused and removed. A single rat can search 1,000 square feet in about 30 minutes, a feat which would take a human operative a full day, and put him or her at terrible risk the whole time. Previously dogs have been used, but they are heavy enough to risk triggering the mines. The rats are 'clicker'-trained to scratch when they detect the right smell. Their trainer was asked why, then, the rats didn't just scratch every few minutes to be given a reward. Their trainer answered, 'That would be human behaviour. Rats are more honest.'

How awful is it in comparison that animals such as dogs and dolphins are also being trained, but to kill rather than save lives? These animals are being sacrificed by having mines strapped to them and then being taught to run or swim under the enemy's machinery. It has always been so in war. Man has always used his animal brothers cruelly.

FINDING THE WAY HOME

So-called owing to their almost supernatural ability to find their way back to their home from strange places, sometimes hundreds of miles away, homing pigeons are more amazing than you might realize. In some experiments they've even been anesthetized for transportation so that there was no possibility of them ever gaining any information about the journey. They've been used for postal services and to carry all kinds of vital messages from as long ago as the sixteenth century, in countries as diverse as ancient Greece and China. They were even used in the 1800s by Paul Reuter to keep stock exchanges up to speed in Brussels and Aachen. It was only in recent years that the police force of India stopped using pigeons to take messages across that vast continent. Even when wounded by bullets, pigeons delivered important messages during the First World War.

When you think about it, it's incredibly amazing how migrating birds also find their way around the world without maps or a compass. They may have an entirely different kind of intelligence to us humans, but who are we to say which is the cleverest?

WHAT'S IN A NAME?
Here is Alice Jean's story.

When I was expecting my first child, like a lot of new mothers-to-be I got a baby name book. Before that I'd never given much thought to the meaning of names. Besides naming my four sons from the book, I looked up the names and meaning of those names for me and my siblings and everyone I knew. *Such an interesting subject,* I thought. There was a time in history when no one had a last name, and then last names were invented to tell one John from another. Their trade or title or location they were from was added on.

Then hubby and I and our four sons moved to a country life and began to raise registered dairy goats. They needed names, of course, to be put on their registry papers, so again I purchased a big fat baby name book and was having fun using all those beautiful girl names I hadn't been able to use for my own children, who were all boys.

Since one must be close to dairy goats so that they're tame and easy to handle later on, we would always pick them up from the day they were born and tell them their name. It's amazing how they caught on so fast and responded to their own name as they were growing up.

There was never any doubt that they knew their own name. It never failed.

Sometimes I would name one Patricia if she was born on or near Saint Patrick's Day, or Esther if she was born near Easter, or Noelle around Christmas. Yes, it always worked, until one particular sweet baby came along whom I tried to name Josie. This one was born on Saint Joseph's day in March, so Josie was my choice. But it certainly was not hers! If she was looking at me I would say, 'Hi Josie,' and she'd quickly turn her head the other way. If I picked her up and said the same thing, her head would turn so quickly away from me that it was almost comical. Hubby suggested I think of another name. I thought and thought and tried out Gracie Jo. The first time I called her that, she actually ran to me. Amazing!

Now I'm the one who tells anyone who will listen that it really doesn't matter what you call your pet as long as you do so with kindness. Animals understand emotions more than words. Something about the tone or sounds of names, though, they pick up on, and maybe we do too, I don't know. Gracie Jo is the only one who reacted this way to a name.

This was unusual because animals don't give each other names, as they only recognize each other by appearance, scent, sound and, of course, energy. But it seems that, just as with people, animals all have their little foibles.

THE DOG WHO DIDN'T WANT TO BE A HOT DOG

The national press in the USA recently reported the story of Max, an 11-year-old chocolate Labrador. His owner had taken Max with her on an errand in the car, but when she got home she forgot he was with her and left him in the car by mistake. It wasn't something she'd usually have done, because it was a very hot day. She got engrossed in chores and with her mind full of other things she forgot completely about Max. About an hour later she heard a car horn blow and interrupted her cleaning to look outside. Not seeing anyone around, she went back in and carried on cleaning. A while later the car horn sounded again, and this time, convinced the sound had come from her own car, she took a closer look and saw Max sitting in the driver's seat, his paw on the horn button. Mortified, she rushed over and got him out of the car. The vet said that the dog had undoubtedly saved his own life that day by having the sense to attract attention with the horn. This behaviour clearly shows an understanding of cause and effect.

This story of war animals comes from Margaret, via Julie, who recently visited her on my behalf at the home where she now resides.

BRAVERY

Margaret Barker is a very special woman. Now frail and elderly, she still had the passion to want to tell me her story. She first became interested in the plight of animals in war many years ago when she met Joey, a horse that was one of the very few to return from the horrors of the battlefields of the First World War, aged then about 30, which is pretty old for a horse, under any circumstances. Margaret was about seven years old at the time and Joey became her friend. For some time she didn't understand why, when being ridden, the bay gelding would always bolt at the sound of bangs or high-pitched noises. Even when he did bolt, Margaret was never afraid and in fact sensed that in running, Joey thought he was looking after her in some way. Of course, to the poor horse the sounds meant 'Run for your life,' and his soldier rider had, I'm sure, always trained him to do just that at the threat of gunfire or mortar.

Margaret loved Joey as soon as she saw him, and although he passed away many years ago, she's aware that he's still with her, and even after all these years he's still looking after her.

Living through man's second conflict, Margaret became aware of the sacrifice made by all concerned but never did she forget the price Joey and millions like him also paid. She recalls finding a book with graphic details of the First World War, among which were pictures of the

11

demise of animals who had been sent to the front. It was at about this time that she came to believe that animals should be commemorated on Remembrance Day, alongside the soldiers for whom they worked and with whom they died.

It was amazing to see what an impact still Joey had on Margaret from so long ago. She went blind 17 years ago and she's often asked me if I think that when she passes over she'll have her sight back. I tell her that I'm convinced her sight will be restored, and that I'm even more convinced that the first spirit she'll see will be Joey – to which she answers with a smile, 'In that case I'm ready to go any time.' Despite being totally blind, Margaret has never lost sight of Joey, the images in the book or her quest to have these animals commemorated.

To love unconditionally/To serve unquestionably/To trust beyond endurance/Bear no malice, trusting loyal and protective/They work, play, live, share, enrich, fight and die for us and with us/Asking little in return, they are the animals/Oh that man could live by this creed also.

When I was a child I loved any film or TV show that featured animals – *Champion the Wonder Horse, Fury, Rin Tin Tin*, etc. I particularly liked cowboy films because horses were my greatest love, and of course these films had horses in virtually every shot. At first I also watched war films, but gradually I became sickened by the fates of the horses in them as they were depicted on the screen. So, when I came across Margaret Barker's quest to recognize animals in war, I was very happy to join in, and I now lay a wreath in my hometown every year on their behalf.

Nowadays, of course, I'm very pleased that there are rules regarding the use of animals in films, and film companies are at pains to point out that no animals are harmed in their filming. I would far rather see an obviously trained roll from a horse that is meant to have fallen heavily, than a gut-wrenching genuine fall in one of the old films.

I remember my nephew laughing at me one day when I got upset watching a fictional film where people were supposedly stranded in an airless room in space and were going to suffocate. The film made an analogy, which would have been clever had the film not been made before the days of computer animation. They showed a toppled fish tank, the fish on the floor gasping for air and dying, just as the people were. I was distraught for the poor fish. My nephew laughingly said, 'Trust you to care more about the fish than the people!' I had to point out to him that the people were just acting, but for the fish it was all too real.

There are some heart-warming steps that have been taken with regard to raising the public's awareness of the amazing ways animals have served mankind in wars. Steven Spielberg has produced a film version of the amazing and incredibly successful stage play *War Horse*, to be released in 2011. It tells the story of 'Albert' and his horse, (coincidentally named 'Joey'). Joey is sold to the cavalry and sent to the trenches of the First World War. Despite being too young to enlist, Albert heads to France to save his friend. The story was originally told in the book of the same name, which was written by Michael Morpurgo.

Also, in 2004 a wonderful sculpture was unveiled in Park Lane, in London. Depicting a life-sized horse and a dog, this is a powerful and moving tribute to all the animals who served, suffered and died in the wars and conflicts of the twentieth century.

CHAPTER 2

Forever Faithful

Pets who return to visit their owners after death

*Many people think animals are not spiritual —
having no spirit or soul. Most think animals are less
intelligent than humans, savage and without society*

or conscience. This is not so.

– GRANDFATHER LEE STANDING BEAR MOORE
(THROUGH HIS FRIEND TAKATOKA)

This will be one of my favourite chapters to write. Since
the publication of *Pets Have Souls Too*, I've been sent hundreds of stories of this nature. It always warms my heart
to read of these animals who have such a deep connection
with their owners that death cannot break it, and they are,
indeed, faithful forever.

FAITHFUL SHADOW
Let's start with Emma's story.

I went to Oxford Castle with a paranormal group a week after I had lost my beloved Golden Retriever, Shadow, my best friend. He looked exactly like the dog on the front of your first pet book so when I saw the book I knew it must be fate that I read it! Shadow died suddenly. He went in for a routine op and the vet found lots of inoperable tumours, so with heavy hearts my family had to make the decision to let him go. I wasn't there at the time, as I was working in a shop. I was on my own and a spirit came to me, and I suddenly knew it was Shadow, but I wouldn't believe it. I said aloud, 'Whoever is there, just cross over, OK?' Then at the end of my shift I went home and my mum told me my Shadow had died.

A week later I was at Oxford Castle and we were using a Ouija board. Shadow came through, he came to me. That morning I'd walked past his picture and had said to him, 'Don't you dare come through. You stay over there!' Nevertheless, the planchette went to the S, then back to the middle, then to the H and it spelled out his name. I said, 'Oh my God! It's him, he's here.' No one believed me. They thought I was mad. They wouldn't even comfort me, but just stood looking at me like I was insane. I was hysterical, trying to ask my dog questions but I couldn't stop crying. I asked him if he was on the other side and he said that he was. I asked him if Granny was with him and he said yes. I said to him, 'It's OK, you can go now,' and just as obedient as he'd always been, he went.

Later on a member of the group asked me, 'How could a dog come through?' She didn't believe me. I imagine she didn't believe that dogs survived death. All I could think of to say to her, in my distress, was that in life he was really intelligent.

Losing an animal to whom you're so close is very traumatic. I think it's very sweet that Shadow tried so hard to comfort his mistress.

FAMILY TIES

There follow a few lovely examples of pets who wouldn't let go, which came from Joanie.

We had a small Yorkie (Yorkshire Terrier) called Pippin, whom we had for 15 years, and then due to ill health we decided it was better for her sake to have her put to sleep. She was taken to the vet's the next morning and quietly and gently put to her last sleep. That evening my husband and I were sitting watching television, when out of the corner of my eye I spotted Pippin's little Yorkie tail disappearing into the bedroom, just as it always had at her usual time of 9 p.m. I remarked to my husband that I thought I had seen Pippin going off to bed, and he answered me with a smile on his face, telling me he'd noticed her, too, disappearing round the corner of his chair beside the fire.

Several years before that, my stepdaughter, Amanda, had passed away. She was only 28 years old when she died and was always close to Pippin. A few days after Amanda died we were interested to see that Pippin kept looking toward the other end of our sitting room as if she could see someone there. She kept walking up and down the room as if looking up at someone. We also felt that there was someone other than us in the room.

We also had a big black fluffy cat called Fudge, at the same time as we had Pippin. The two animals were very close, to the point that they would curl up with each other on the settee. Fudge was put to sleep at the grand old age of 17 years old. Like most cats, Fudge loved to catch birds, which always upset us so we bought a small bell to slot on his collar to warn the birds away when he was approaching. The evening of the day he was put to sleep we heard his bell tinkling around the kitchen where he usually slept. Also during the night after we retired to bed. This lasted for a few days, then stopped.

My hubby passed away four years ago, and even now when I have received messages from him, it's always mentioned that there's a small Yorkshire Terrier by his side.

It's very comforting to know that we'll all be reunited with our very special pets as well as our loved ones after we pass over.

BOGART'S GOODBYE

Lynda wrote to tell me this next story.

Let me tell you what happened to my family some 11 years ago. My sister's husband died from a brain aneurysm. He was only in his early fifties and his children were still at school. It was a traumatic time for everyone, especially for my sister, and my mum, who loved him like a son. We all felt his passing, but we didn't realize how much the family dog, a mini Foxie (Fox Terrier) named Bogart, was affected by his loss. When Greg was alive he used to take Bogart for long, wonderful walks and sometimes, when it was a hot day, would even smuggle him into the local pub for a refreshing pint. After Greg's death, Bogart would climb up on my sister's chest and would comfort her with his presence. Some time after the funeral, the family decided to go to the cemetery to pay

Greg a visit. Bogart came along. The cemetery is spread over a vast area, and we searched for a tree which was our marker. Finding the tree was no problem, but we all agreed that we had no idea where Greg was buried. It was just row upon row upon row of plots. We opened the car door and out shot Bogart. He's only little, so he quickly disappeared from our sight. We decided to search for Bogart before restarting our search for Greg's grave. Then we heard it – a terrible and distressed howling that was coming from one of the rows. We followed the noise and, to our astonishment and shock, found little Bogart on Greg's plot, all four paws planted firmly, head raised high and howling over and over again. At the time we were all very frightened and distressed by what we saw. There was Greg's little mate, who'd not only found him amongst thousands of plots but was crying out to him at the top of his voice.

Jenny, why did this happen? How did he find Greg, as he was buried in a family plot and the concrete covering him was well and truly set? My sister never took Bogart back to the cemetery. Bogart's coming up to 12 – do you think we should take him again to see his dad?

My answer to Lynda was this:

Gosh, your story about Bogart made me cry, but it is beautiful. My feeling is that Bogart felt he never got to say goodbye to his dad. I also feel that perhaps Greg's spirit was hanging around the grave, waiting for the same chance, and certain that at some point you'd bring his boy there. I feel this strongly and am sure that what Bogart could sense was not Greg's earthly remains, but the essence of his spirit. Most likely if you took him there again, he would be calm, now that he's said goodbye. As Bogart ages, his connection to Greg will strengthen, and you can be sure that when it's Bogart's time to go, Greg will be waiting for him with open arms. Thank you so much for allowing my readers to share this poignant story.

SOUL SISTER

A woman who goes by the name 'Lil' Aug' sent me this amazing story.

When I was a little girl I would draw pictures of a German Shepherd, a wolf-like dog with bright eyes and perky ears. I didn't know why I was drawing these pictures, but I just felt a need to. I told everyone that this was going to be my future dog one day.

Years later, my mother and father brought a puppy home with them. As soon as I saw this little wolf-like pup, my eyes lit up in excitement. I felt an instant attachment to this puppy, as though I'd known her before. We called her Mandy.

As Mandy grew up, she resembled the drawings I used to make as a little girl. She even had the same bright eyes, so much so that my mother used to nickname her Bright Eyes. Mandy was a very intelligent dog. We think she had some wolf breeding in her. A woman we met in Canada who raised wolves mentioned that to us once. She said Mandy's mannerisms were just like the wolf pups'.

Some time later, around 2007, we had to put Mandy to sleep. Too many over-the-counter snacks we gave her had brought on diabetes. We didn't know she had it, but eventually she wasn't even able to walk any longer. While I was at work that dark day, I felt Mandy's presence with me outside my workplace. I thought how odd that was, as she wasn't supposed to be euthanized until later that afternoon. I still felt her presence with me, sitting with me on the pavement during my 12:30 lunch break. I called my mother, who confirmed that they'd decided to put Mandy to sleep at 12 o'clock. I cried my eyes out in grief.

Months later, around 2 a.m. one January night, I was awakened from my sleep by some strong energy in our home. While lying in bed with my eyes open, I heard Mandy's familiar wolf-like howl downstairs in our living room, I didn't know at the time that my mother (who sleeps downstairs) had also heard her. I sent out a thought to Mandy and called out to her in my mind. I said, 'Mandy, if that is you, come upstairs and be with me!' Suddenly I felt a rush of energy near the left side of my bed. I felt this feeling of excitement and relief and joy. And I felt her lick my face – not exactly a physical sensation but still an energy-like feeling that a dog was licking my face. I sensed her emotion. I fell back asleep with a smile on my face, but never shared this experience with anyone in my family, including my mother.

Some weeks later my mother blurted out in the car that she'd heard Mandy howl in the living room some weeks before. I stared at her with my mouth open while my father joked that she was losing it mentally. I interrupted and told her how I'd heard Mandy, too. We both looked at each other and realized from that day forward that animals have souls and that they live on as humans do. Mandy was my soul sister. Whether in another life, or in the heavenly realms of the Great Spirit, I know that we knew each other before, and we'll see each other again.

DOING THE RIGHT THING

Shelley Kaehr, PhD, told me about this awakening which the death of a pet brought to her.

I've loved and lost many pets through the years, and one incident that sticks out most in my mind is about a little Cocker Spaniel named Crystal, who belonged to my then husband. He'd had Crystal since childhood and, shortly after we were married, my husband's parents decided to bring her from Kansas to Texas to live with us. The trouble was that by then Crystal was very old, sick and blind, and when she arrived at our house she had no idea where she was or who we were. By that time she was thin, shaking and completely incontinent and, unfortunately, due to the mess she would make we had to keep her outside much of the time, which literally broke my heart. I remember many nights sitting at the kitchen table crying over that poor little dog. We absolutely did not know what to do for her.

A couple of months passed and it became apparent that Crystal was getting worse and seemed to be in pain. She limped on her legs and, although she never complained, it was obviously getting unbearable. I took her to the vet who, of course, suggested we put her to sleep. I'd never had to do anything like that before. My pets normally either died of natural causes or got lost over the years, and I was not sure what to think about such drastic measures. I came home and told my husband about it and we cried some more, wondering all the while what would be the best course of action. I spent a long time thinking about this issue, and whether or not it's OK to assist our fuzzy friends in their transition. I know this is a controversial subject for some and that there are many opinions about the topic.

After thinking it over, I've come to feel we take better care of our pets at times than we do each other. There is a time to live and a time to die, and unfortunately, since our animals are innocents, there is no real way for them to communicate with us to let us know what they need, how they feel and what they would want to have happen at the end of their lives. Personally, I feel some of the treatments we give our animals to sustain their lives are inhumane because they have no way to understand what is being done to them or why. They only know they are away from us, the ones they love, and being tortured and hurt by needles, tubes and treatments which eventually will not avoid the inevitable.

My mom and I took Crystal to the vet late one morning and sat with her as the vet administered the shot. Her breathing slowed down and I could see her pain was gone. Right at the end, she opened her eyes, looked up at me and seemed to say, 'Thank you.' It's a blink in time I will never forget. It was a good death, a peaceful transition.

Within moments she was gone, and that's when the miracle happened: I suddenly heard a whooshing sound as her soul departed from her body. At first I couldn't believe it, but then the room was filled with peace, and I felt glad she was finally at rest and could run and play in the grassy fields of Heaven. At that moment, any doubt as to whether or not I'd done the right thing melted away. She was at peace, out of pain and no longer suffering. It's tough to say goodbye, harder to let go, but in the end it brought peace to both of us.

I've spent time working as a hospice volunteer and experienced many unusual and mystical experiences in my life, but of all of the things I've seen, I think this experience with Crystal was one of the most important. It showed me that we really are unlimited souls who survive bodily death and that these forms we take while here in the physical are not who we truly are. We are infinite and so are our furry friends. We will all meet again one day in the energetic life of the hereafter, and what a gloriously happy day that will be!

Shelley makes a very good point with her story. I often have people write and tell me about their sick pets, and how they can't bear to let the animal go. Or they write to tell me they did make this very tough decision and are now wracked with guilt as to whether they did the right thing. I went through the same with my doggy soulmate, Ace. I kept putting off having her put to sleep because I couldn't bear the thought of being without her, of being 'responsible' for her death, or of letting her go prematurely and living with the guilt of that. I worried that because she still sometimes seemed to be enjoying herself I should let her continue. It was my son, Phillip, who put things into perspective for me when he said, 'Just because she's able to smile now and then, it doesn't mean her life is worth living the rest of the time.' In the wild, sick, old or injured animals are quickly despatched by Nature. Having taken animals out of the wild and tamed them, we owe it to them to take the place of Nature and, when the time is right and they no longer enjoy life, we have to stop their suffering. If a dog can't run and play and interact with the family, then it can't continue being a dog. If a cat can't hunt or wrestle or pounce, then it can't continue to be a cat. If a horse can't run from fears, real or imaginary, or kick up its heels in joy, then it can't continue to be a horse. This applies to all animals and their natural behaviour. Someone, sometime, has to draw a line, and that duty falls to us.

A PIG BY ANY OTHER NAME

To cheer you up I'm going to include this funny and beautiful story from Maggie.

A few years back a lovely woman came for a reading. Before she arrived I'd been thinking of pigs. For some reason they simply kept popping into my head. After the opening intro, a 'How are you?' sort of thing, we settled down to her reading. One of the first things I do is go out there and find someone to talk to me. Usually a passed relative will come through and validate a few things, which sets the client at ease and the reading goes from there. This time, however, no matter what I did, all I kept seeing was a smiling pig. So after about five minutes of nothing but pig, I had to ask it what it was doing there, and I was given the name of Henry. I breathed a huge sigh of relief, thinking, *Now we're getting somewhere.* So I asked the client if the name Henry meant anything.

She took a huge breath and nearly shouted, 'Yes!'

So far so good. Only all I saw was a pig. Smiling at me.

So I quietly said, 'But he's a pig.'

'Yes! Yes!' she cried.

I said, 'A real pig, not a character trait.'

'Yes!' again.

And then it flowed. Henry was the most beloved, pampered pig you could ever have met. He led me through how she had bought what was meant to be a pot-bellied little boy and ended up with a huge pot-bellied boy. He talked of his skin problem, and how they had to change shampoo so many times before importing one that suited his skin, and of his love of candy floss and apples, mostly in the same dish. Then he continued to describe the events that had happened in her life since he passed over. He did mention that he had a bowel twist which caused trauma, with the ultimate result of him having to be put down. All of this amazing two-hour chat turned out to be accurate.

And I didn't eat bacon for a long while afterwards.

I loved that story because so often the letters and emails I get sent are all about dogs, cats and recognized 'pet' material. Pigs have souls too!

BIG CAT!

Here's Lisa's story about the comfort she still gets from a cat no longer with her except in spirit.

Our beloved cat, Tara, was a bit of a wanderer, and one evening in 1996 he was knocked down and killed. We were very distraught and buried him in our front garden. His brother is still alive to this day. We decided straight away to get another cat, and went to the shelter, as we always do, believing that it's better to home an unwanted animal than to pay for a pedigree and encourage their breeding. We went into the cattery that day, and there among an array of young cats we saw this black beauty who pushed her way to the front, her eyes looking as though she knew us. In effect, she picked us! From day one she developed her own personality and the characteristics that made 'Panther' the extremely special cat she was.

She developed a taste for cheese-and-onion crisps, which she would even gently take from my mouth. She also had a taste for Chinese food! One day for a joke we asked if she wanted either cat food or curry. Her eyes lit up at the mention of curry! At mealtimes she would come running as soon as she heard the knocking sound I made with my knife. She waited patiently for her treat. Mealtimes thus became very funny, as if she knew in advance what was coming.

She always curled up on the quilt next to me and seemed to talk to me with her eyes. Like most cats she would quite often sleep for long periods. She loved to roll over and let me stroke her belly, often chirping at me. She also loved playing with leaves in the wind on the lawn, but all the time she would keep checking to see where I was. She sometimes even accompanied me into the bathroom, where she'd lie behind my head and enjoy my taste of music, such as Status Quo, as I soaked in the hot water. She even seemed to dance with me. In effect, we became inseparable.

Sadly she was taken from us in March 2009 at the age of 13, following a short illness. She died in my bedroom, with me holding her paw, and even now I well up at the thought of that time. However, I feel she's never really left me. I get a breeze from where she lay on my bed, which is stronger when she answers me. She lets me know she's still with me all the time. When we go out for coffee her head appears to be etched in the foam in the cup as if to say, 'I'm with you.' The impression of her shape regularly appears on the cushion and quilt as if she's still here. She's around me constantly and playing with me, and I find her messages a comfort and remain fiercely loyal to her memory.

Our pets seem to know when we can't possibly let go of them. They come back to bring us comfort when we need it and stay around until we're ready to move on or they can guide us onto a new path; this is one of the things that prove to me that they do have souls.

CHAPTER 3

Guardians Who Never Leave Us

Pets who have reappeared after death to protect their owners

Some pets that we're very close to contain a spark of our soul, and as such we cannot be severed from them. They will always be there next to us.

— JENNY SMEDLEY

WOZA!

Hayley lives in South Africa and sent me this truly remarkable story.

My first story starts on New Year's Eve in 1985. I had seen an advert in the newspaper for a ten-month-old pony, free to a good home. We were living in a residential area but on over an acre of ground, and my dad had applied to the council and been granted permission to keep a horse on the property. We travelled nearly 40km to meet the horsebox that had brought the pony, called Storm, from his farm 300km away. We then transferred him to our box and took him home. He'd never been handled by people so it was all a bit traumatic for him. Once we got to our place I released him into the garden and spent a bit of time attempting to approach him without much success. Later that afternoon we had to go out and someone forgot to shut the gate. When I got home, Storm was gone. I was devastated. We searched the neighbourhood and eventually decided to take a run out on the main road about 1km from the house just to see if he'd headed toward farmland. We'd gone 8km when I saw him on the side of the road.

Obviously I couldn't catch him so we herded him into an enclosed field and spoke to the farmer who owned it about returning the following day to catch him, box him and take him home. The farmer was great, putting out water and hay for Storm, and we went home. At 11:45 that night there was a knock on our door. It being New Year's we figured it was a neighbour coming to wish us well. It was the neighbour, but she said to me, 'Is that your horse outside, banging on your gate, trying to get onto the property?' Of course I didn't think it could be because as far as I knew he was nearly 10km away, the other side of a residential suburb and then across a main highway, but went to bring the horse into safety anyway. Blow me down if it wasn't Storm! He was standing there pleased as punch. I walked straight up to him, opened the gate and in he walked like he'd been there his entire life. From that minute I could handle him. He came into the house up the back stairs, came to a whistle and was literally my constant companion. He was trained to voice commands, never had a bit in his mouth, and when it came time to ride him, off we went as if he'd done it his whole life.

On 25 September 1987 Storm looked off-colour, so I phoned the vet who was at an emergency, described his symptoms and the vet said he'd come out first thing in the morning as it didn't sound serious. Well, I bedded Storm down but my parents wouldn't let me spend the night with him as he wasn't sick as such. I got up the next day and he'd just died. The vet did a post-mortem and found that Storm had died from massive liver failure, which no one could explain to me. I honestly nearly died, too. I lost 8kg in two weeks, I had such terrible guilt.

Then in 1991 I was having a quiet drink in a pub nearly 2,000km away from where this happened and a lady walked up to me, looked me in the eyes and said, 'Storm says it wasn't your fault!' and she walked away...

In October 1987 a farrier friend of mine took me to work with him one day. On the farm where he was working there was a litter of six-week-old German Shepherd puppies. The owner said to me, 'Don't go near the runt, there's something wrong with her. She was born 14 hours after the rest of the litter and she's aggressive.'

Well, I couldn't believe a six-week-old pup could possibly be aggressive, but when they approached her she snapped and snarled like a wild thing. I sat down and played with the pups, and the next thing the 'aggressive runt' is sitting on my lap! They couldn't believe it when I played with her and she was so sweet. I got a phone call two weeks later and the owner asked me if I wanted her as she was going to be euthanized because no one could approach her. Obviously I said yes immediately. I really needed someone to put my love into as my life was so empty without Storm. They had already named her, because of her temperament, and when I asked what they'd called her, they told me her name was Stormi...

She was a very old soul and never had to be taught anything. She was a perfect lady and loved everyone.

When she was just 14 weeks old, I got up in the morning and went to wake her and found that she'd died in the night. Post-mortem: massive liver failure.

Move on to 2009 … I went for a walk with a group of Rhodesian Ridgeback people in a park. In comes a lady I'd never met before, whose name was Cheryl, and with her were three puppies. I was not in the market for another dog! Whenever Cheryl called them, she said 'Woza!', which is a Zulu word meaning 'come here', and this was just one of her many eccentricities! Anyway, at the end of the walk she approached me and asked if I'd be interested in the pup that had a black mask. I was very restrained and didn't snatch him and run! We went home and discussed it and then went to collect him the following day. The entire time we sat in the kitchen having coffee and discussing the terms of ownership, he sat framed in the window on a bed, watching. He was going to be called Zorro, due to the mask – and it means fox (my surname) in Spanish. Cheryl's husband called him 'Bakkies', which is an Afrikaans word that means face or mask, due to his black face, or 'Mombakkies', which is literally mask or, rudely, face ache! Anyway, Bakkies he became because Zorro just didn't fit him. Again, this was a dog to whom I had to teach nothing. He was a very serious, very, very old soul and my constant companion. When I fed the horses and donkeys he'd carry the bucket of food for me. He was a dog everyone loved.

There's an autistic girl, who is about 20, whose mom does dog training with me. Lauren sits and watches the class. Bakkies would go sit next to her with his head in her lap. The first time she ever spoke in front of people other than her family was to him, and then to me, to ask about him. He was just that sort of dog. Whenever we went for a walk he'd seek out empty cans of lager and drink the dregs. He had a real taste for lager! He was six months old when I came home one day to find that he stank like the cellar in a pub. He'd found two crates of beer in my laundry room on top of the freezer, knocked them down and, between him and two others, had opened and drunk almost the whole contents of 32 cans! When the vet finished laughing he assured me the dogs would be fine but would have a horrible hangover the following day.

The following day Bakkies was really not well. I had to go to dog training that evening and thought I'd leave him at home as he was unwell. However, he really wanted to come so off we went. On my way home, at nearly 8 o'clock at night, in the pitch dark, I had to stop at a very slow-moving traffic light. The dogs were lying down fast asleep in the back. Next thing I knew this hand came through my window and grabbed me by the throat and was going for my car keys. There was another man on the other side trying to get that door open, too. Now, the best result would have been for just my car to have been taken. Unfortunately I was more likely to have been abducted and all that goes with that. The next thing I knew, the most terrifying sight I've ever seen in my life came over the back of my seat and attacked the man who had his hand around my throat. Six-month-old Bakkies attacked him so viciously that there was blood all over the car. Luckily both men ran off into the night and I managed to drive home.

I had just two weeks of bragging rights – and you better believe I boasted about having my life saved by this baby. Then I was outside with him and he suddenly screamed and fell down, screaming all the while. Within 30 seconds my Bakkies was dead. The post-mortem showed he had died from an extremely rare non-congenital heart defect. The vets were amazed and had to consult specialists around the world to put a name to it.

The night after he died, once I eventually slept, I had a dream. Bakkies came from behind one of my outbuildings with the tiniest, funniest looking, weirdest coloured little Ridgeback bitch puppy (I'm not a bitch fan) with a red ribbon round her neck. He 'told' me her name was

'Mouse', and if I didn't believe him I was to 'ask Scout' (my African grey parrot). Then he walked away and left this little scrap sitting in front of me, staring up at me. I woke up and I was devastated. I got up and went through to the living room. As my daughter and I walked in, my parrot looked at me and said 'Woza' (the word Cheryl used to call her pups) as clear as a bell, even though he'd never heard that word in his life.

In October I got a call from Cheryl, inviting me to go look at a litter of one of her bitch's pups. They all had homes but she said I should just go and see them. We went out and there was this little scrap with a red ribbon. It took all my power not to burst into tears, as I knew they all had homes, but there was 'Mouse' clear as day. I honestly thought my heart was going to break. The entire time we sat inside she sat framed in the window looking in, exactly as Bakkies had done before her. I didn't say anything as I didn't want Cheryl to feel she had to either give me the pup or disappoint me because she couldn't give me the pup.

When I got into the car, much to my husband's panic, I burst into tears. I told him, 'I've just seen Mouse, but she's got a home!' He said, 'Listen, I don't know which one she was, but Cheryl asked me if you'd be interested in the little girl with the red ribbon.' Apparently she'd asked him to broach the subject with me as she didn't want me to take a pup if it wasn't the right one! Now I have 'Mhousse' (spelled this way for numerology reasons).

I know Bakkies is still around. Scout regularly says 'Woza' now, but only when I'm feeling a bit low or sad. A while after Bakkies died the light above 'his' chair started to come on and off randomly. My husband is an electrician and has checked it, to curb my still present doubts, and there's no fault in it. If I take photos of other dogs sleeping on 'Bakkies' chair', there is always an orb there or thereabouts. I'd never taken a photo of an orb before so when I saw the first one, two weeks after he died, I thought something was wrong with the camera.

This story made me cry and smile. It's very sad that poor Hayley seemed to have lost so many much loved pets, but they all seem to have come to her for a purpose. It was hard to decide which chapter to put this in, but I put it here because I feel that the original Storm came back in several different species' bodies in order to be there at that moment, in that situation, with Hayley, to save her as Bakkies did. Hopefully she'll have a long and trouble-free association with Mhousse now that incident has passed. In fact there was an addition to this story concerning Scout, the parrot. He's recently started making the sounds of the toys that used to belong to Hayley's pets that have passed over. Hayley was thrilled at this contact, but worried that it meant her pets were unhappy or being held back by her. I told her:

It doesn't mean they're not happy or not moving on either, because all of us, whether we're living here at the time or not, keep a part of ourselves in spirit. That part can always be in touch and it wouldn't matter if your pets had moved into new bodies – a part of them could still connect with you. They're sending the messages because they love you and have found a way to talk to you.

TAKING CARE OF THINGS

Stephanie told me this lovely story about a dog who wanted to make sure that after she died her owners would find another dog to love and wouldn't leave until they did.

We adopted Lucy, a four-year-old Cocker Spaniel who was looking for a new home after her owners split. Tony, my husband, and I took her into our home and our hearts and for almost five years we lived as one. We had both finished work a year prior to Lucy arriving and had all the time in the world to help her settle into her new home – which was quite a task, such was her loyalty to her first owners.

We adored her, and she adored us. She was never more than a few feet away from me at any time. Then suddenly, one June day, she developed breathing problems which turned out to be the symptoms of serious heart failure, and she was not expected to live the night. Miraculously she did and, with medication, life returned to normal within a few short days.

All seemed well, and then on 10 December my husband was out and Lucy was reposing on a cream velvet armchair. We had a glass door and a glass window in the lounge, looking into the hall. Suddenly Lucy stood up on the chair and wagged her tail in absolute joy. I saw that she was looking out of the door, and whatever it was she was looking at then must have moved, as she shifted her gaze to the window. Sure that my husband had returned home, I left the room to greet him, only to find that there was no one there. I was seriously spooked by this, and when he eventually did return I told him I feared Lucy was going to die and that someone had come for her. That was a Wednesday, and on the Saturday she died. We're convinced some person or some animal had come for her. Whoever it was caused utter joy, which is some comfort.

After we'd buried her in the garden, my husband was

making good the ground, re-laying the turf as I watched anxiously from the house, and to my amazement I could see that he was smiling. When he came in he said that the strangest thing had happened. Lucy had a special song that he often sang to her, and she would join in by howling, and we would laugh. She loved this and would sometimes initiate the song by making strange sounds and looking at us expectantly, which was a signal for the song to begin! He said that as he was tending the grave, this song came to him clearly, hence his smile.

During that day I spoke of my envy that she'd made contact with him. We went to bed, for the first dreadful night without our girl, and as I fell asleep I dreamed, but it was more than a dream. I was back in the lounge, Lucy was on the aforementioned chair, and although the room was dark, where she was it was bright light. She was licking and fussing me in joyful reunion, but I knew it was not forever and that she would go again. Suddenly we were by the fireplace, which opened up into a dark tunnel, and she disappeared into it. A clock on the mantelpiece tilted forward and a door at the front of it swung open at this moment.

I awoke with a start; my heart was pounding and I was crying. I woke Tony to tell him I'd seen Lucy. He said that in his prayers moments before I had the dream he'd spoken to Lucy, asking her to visit me as I really needed her to. It settled me enormously and made me feel so happy – for a short time. In discussion, we decided that the tilting of the clock and the opening of the door were meant to signify it was time to go, or that her time had come.

During the course of the next week we made enquiries to find another puppy. I was in contact with a breeder who told me she had only one left. I was concerned in case it was the runt of the litter, but she said it wasn't – the pup just did not run forward to prospective buyers but certainly was not weak or timid. All the other puppies mobbed the visitors, but for some reason she just sat back and watched.

We duly went for a viewing and I looked expectantly for a puppy in the background but could see none. I asked the owner which was the available puppy and, surprised, she laughingly said that it was the one Tony was holding. She had run straight to him! Again, we believe that Lucy had contacted the puppy and told her to hold back until we came. Of course we bought her.

Nothing more happened, other than the song I mentioned previously came to both of our minds on a quite regular basis that first year, and we knew Lucy was making contact. And on one occasion Tony had got up to use the bathroom during the night. We live in a bungalow and he had glanced across the dark hall into the lounge and seen Lucy sitting on the back of her chair as she always had done. We accepted that she was visiting us.

As Lucy had died, Tony had picked up a curl of her fur at the vet's. I'd wrapped it up in tissue, folded it over and over again until it was about two inches square, put it into a little suede jewellery bag, tied it tightly and put it under my pillow, where it had remained for a year. On the first anniversary of Lucy's death I decided I would look at the fur again, just to feel the softness once more. I untied the bag and carefully unfolded the tissue, which was almost impossible as I had been lying on it for a year, but I managed to do it and, to my utter shock, there was nothing there, no trace of any fur ever having been there, nothing, zilch. I stared open-mouthed and the only explanation we could think was that Lucy had taken it simply as a way of making contact on that day. As we went to bed that night, Tony asked me if Molly (our new dog) was with me, because he'd just seen a dog at the end of the lounge out of the corner of his eye, but Molly had been with me all the time, so it was clearly another visit.

During that night in bed, I woke up and was mulling over the issue of the fur in the little pouch bag, wondering if there could be any other explanation that I was missing, although I knew for sure in my heart that Lucy had taken it – but you know you try not to fool yourself, you want to be sure. As I thought, I reached under the pillow for the now empty pouch and withdrew my hand quickly as it felt so hot. If I could describe the intensity of the heat I'd say that, had I looked at it, I would have expected it to be glowing, that was the strength of the heat emanating from it. It served to confirm to us that Lucy truly had removed the fur as a way of making contact and that her energy was still with the bag in which it had been for some hours afterwards.

Over the next few days I of course tried to re-create the incident, reaching under my pillow, making sure that the bag was under my head, but on each occasion the bag was cold. Since that time, there has been nothing else. It would seem that Lucy saw us through that first awful year, got us happily loving our new Molly, and then moved on.

SHADOW ANIMALS

Sallyanne's story is about a very special dog who saved her from harm.

I always played in the woods when I was a kid. I guess it was safer back then, but apart from my parents telling me 'not to talk to strangers' I was pretty much left alone.

I was a bit of a loner, too, preferring to play in the fields among the cows, which never troubled me. When I went to the woods I was never scared of the trees, and I was really puzzled that some of the other kids were. They saw faces in the trunks, they said, bad spirits that would reach out gnarly arms at night and grab them, then drag them down into the earth or into the tree's mouth. I thought they were nuts. I'd even walk in the woods at twilight, and I was never scared – well, not of the trees anyway. For most of my childhood I had my dog Tallow to keep me company and keep me safe. We grew up together, us having got her when I was only two years old. What I'm about to tell you happened at a time when Tallow was recovering from a small operation and so couldn't come out with me. I'd given her a hug that morning, told her it was only for a while and gone out alone. I got playing and forgot the time and it was getting dusky as I set off home. I was almost clear of the woods when I started hearing twigs snapping and footsteps. I knew there were some campers nearby, but I wasn't scared of them and I thought it was one of them out rabbiting or something. But after a while the sounds started to come from in front instead of behind me and I knew there was something fishy about this person stalking me, sneaking round to cut me off. When he stepped out of the bushes in front of me I wanted to scream, but nothing would come out. Besides, I was too far away from the houses for anyone to hear me. The man was about 30, scruffy-looking and definitely up to no good. He smiled and walked toward me, herding me into a bramble patch. Soon there would be no escape – I knew that but I couldn't run and was forced to just keep backing away. I felt the thorny bushes at my back and knew I'd run out of space.

'Come on, sweetheart, don't be shy,' the man said. His words opened my throat and I was able to scream one word, 'Tallow!'

I don't know why I did that, since I knew my little guardian couldn't hear me from where she lay on her bed at home. I reckon the man knew she wasn't around, too, because he smiled again. He reached out his arms, coming to me, and then suddenly a shadow appeared behind him. It flew through the air and then it and the man went tumbling to the ground. Now it was his turn to yell. It all happened so fast that I can't honestly say for sure what I saw, as I ran past him as fast as I could. I didn't stop running until I crashed through the back door of home and fell to my knees beside Tallow, who greeted me enthusiastically with her wet tongue. I know what it was, though. Somehow my dearest, bravest dog had heard my cry and had sent her shadow to save me. I never, ever told my family what happened, and I never will, but I'm sharing this story with you, Jenny, because I think it's important that people know. I never went into those woods without Tallow again. .

I've heard of shadow animals before, although usually they seem to refer to animals who have passed over and returned in this form. This is the only story so far of a dog who transformed into a 'shadow' while she was still alive. If you have heard of another, please let me know!

This reminds me a little of my old dog, Sally. I never actually saw her as a shadow, but this ability in Tallow might explain something very odd that used to happen. Sally was sometimes shut away indoors while I and/or other children played out in the road with a ball. Sally's bed was in the outhouse, which only had one window quite high up, so she couldn't see us. Quite often, almost always in fact, sooner or later the ball would disappear into the thick bushes and hedgerow opposite our house, which was several hundred yards long and about 30 feet thick, and despite our best efforts it would seemingly be lost for good. The other children would immediately start calling for Sally, and if I wasn't with them already they'd knock on the door for me to bring her out. Then Sally would simply disappear into the hedge, without any instructions, and always, without fail, reappear in seconds with the ball in her mouth. It was odd because I don't believe she found it by smell, as it could have smelled of any one of a dozen children, and she never hesitated, never sniffed the air, but just went directly to the ball as if she'd seen it not only go into the undergrowth, but had even seen exactly where it landed. I have to wonder now, after hearing about Tallow, whether Sally too was able to send her shadow where she herself couldn't go.

FREE SPIRIT

Brenda sent me this story.

My pet dog Tinker was really special to me. He slept on my bed every night and 'guarded' me from even my parents if they popped in to check on me! We lived in the country about half a mile from the main road and local bus stop. My mum used to take the dogs (we had two) at night to meet my older sister off the last bus. Tinker had a habit of 'slipping his collar'. He was used to roaming free at home and hated having to wear one.

On this particular evening, Mum was going to meet my sister off the bus and I had this awful premonition that Tinker would die if she took him with her. I pleaded with her not to take him, and just to take our other dog, but she insisted, telling me not to be so silly. I just knew I wouldn't be seeing him again. That night, as my sister got off the bus across the road, Tinker got excited seeing her and slipped his collar and ran across the road to greet her, right in front of a tanker.

I still feel him with me sometimes at night when I'm in bed. It feels like I can't push my feet down the bed because he's sitting on them, and I just know it is him with me. I lost Tinker when I was only about 14 but I remember that night as if it were yesterday, and I know that Tinker never has to wear a collar now.

THE LITTLE MOUSE WHO COULD

Jason's story (I've changed Jason's name because his parents didn't want to be connected to the story, for understandable reasons).

People used to laugh at me because I always had a pet mouse or two with me. Of course some people didn't laugh; they screamed when two little round ears and a twitchy nose peeked out of my pocket unexpectedly. They were the saddos, though, not me. I always had a lot of mice – sometimes there were upwards of 20 or so in my bedroom. I liked to give them the run of my room but my mom was always worried they were going to get out and run riot all round the house. I wouldn't have cared but I knew that she'd have been tempted to set traps, and I wouldn't have liked that at all.

People thought I couldn't possibly tell all my mice apart or know their names, but of course I did. To me every one was an individual with different ways and a different face or body markings. My favourite was one I called Jerry. Not original, I know, but there you go. It was when I was about 12 that a weird thing happened which made Mom love my mice, too. Dad was a smoker, Mom too, although she was always trying to stop. She used to beg dad to stop, saying she couldn't do it if he didn't, but he wouldn't hear of it. I hated the smoke and it made me spend more time in my room with my mice.

When Jerry got sick I was really upset because he was my pal. I used to take him everywhere with me. He was the only black-and-white mouse I ever owned – and you'll see why that's important in a minute. At the time I had him, stocks were a bit low and all the other mice where white, black or brown, solid colours. I saved Jerry from a pet shop where he was in a tiny cage and had pulled some of his own fur out, he was so miserable. I swear he yelled at me to take him home. Well, I did anyway. Jerry was with me practically 24 hours a day. Even at school he knew to keep down low in my pocket and not peep out, so I usually got away with having him there. Anyway, he got sick and he died. I don't want to talk too much about that, but for weeks I could still feel him in my pocket.

One night everyone was asleep. I didn't know it but my dad had had fallen asleep in his chair. He'd woken up later and gone to bed, forgetting that he'd had a cigarette in his hand when he fell asleep. The cigarette must have slowly burned away smouldering in the chair, until it finally set it on fire after Dad had gone to bed. I was asleep like all the family, until I felt a tail twitching on my lips. I opened my eyes and there stood Jerry, on my nose, staring into my eyes, and I could still feel his tail flipping back and forth over my mouth. His one-black-and-one-white ears showed clearly in the light from the street. Next thing I knew I could smell burning. Jerry just vanished at that point and I leapt out of bed. There was a wisp of smoke curling under the door. I started yelling and my parents woke up. They came into my room, saying the stairs were alight, and we all crawled out the window onto the porch roof and then slid down to the ground in our nightclothes. I had, of course, stopped to grab the cage of my mice before I'd agree to leave. I looked back into the room before I jumped, worrying that somehow I'd left one black-and-white mouse behind. But I couldn't see anything, and anyway I just knew that mouse had to be a ghost. We lost the house, but we didn't lose each other. I was surprised when my mom believed my story. Dad said he didn't, no way, but he gave up smoking.

Heroes come in all shapes and sizes, but I have to admit this is the first and, so far, only heroic mouse I've been told about. I'm sure you'll let me know if you know different! It seems that Jerry was one for paying his debts, and he saved Jason in return for being saved from the pet shop.

CHAPTER 4

I'm Back!

Pets who have regenerated and come back to their owners in a new body, sometimes even in the body of a different species

All of our souls were once contained in the bodies of animals. It's only with this preparation that we can ever hope to remain spiritual and human at the same time.

– JENNY SMEDLEY

It fascinates me because my main subject in my spiritual life has always been reincarnation, that most of the stories sent to me about pets just happen to come under this umbrella. Perhaps I just attract them, or perhaps the subject is becoming more relevant in this world we live in.

CATS AND DOGS
Kathleen shares her story.

Mork, my special cat, came to me as the lone survivor of a litter of kittens. He seemed to be imbued with an especially strong connection to life, for he survived the loss of his mother and all of his litter-mates by the time he was just two weeks old. I bottle-fed him after his mother passed on, and took care of all of his needs, and he survived against all odds. Perhaps the bond between us was established at this time. But there was a definite bond there. He became more like a child than a pet, and even my children to this day think of him as being more like a brother, not just a pet. His life was nearly taken from us so many times during the 18 years we were together. He got in a scrap with another cat, perhaps a wild animal, which left him with a raging infection that nearly took his life. I nursed him through that. One fateful day years later I rescued Mork from the jaws of a neighbour's dog. He was so severely injured (internally nearly bitten in two) that he had to have extensive surgery after a frantic rush to the emergency vet through a snowstorm. He miraculously recovered. Some years later I found him out in the garden in a secluded spot very near death's door. I scooped him up and took him to the Veterinary

Hospital. The diagnosis was severe anaemia. I took the poor half-dead fellow home. He was so near death that his body temperature was low and he was semi-conscious and delirious. He very nearly passed away that night. I sat up with him all night long, keeping him warm and hydrated, and when morning came I knew my efforts were not futile because he wasn't in renal failure! He got up and promptly peed on my basket of clean laundry. I was overjoyed!

Life settled down for a few years after that and we enjoyed Mork's elder years with us.

One day the vet told me that Mork's kidneys were failing. I asked if they did kidney transplants on cats. Mork was like my child and I would have done anything to keep him living as long as possible. The vet told me they didn't do them. (Shortly after this, veterinary medicine made advances in that area. Too late for my Morkey, though.) We faced the inevitable and about a year after the dire prognosis, Mork's kidneys indeed began to fail. He passed quietly in my bedroom and we buried him in a prominent spot in the garden near the front door.

His passing left a big hole in our family. We had gotten a kitten shortly after getting the dire prognosis of kidney failure for Mork. We named the new kitten Korkey. She was an orange long-haired cat similar to Mork, and she was charming and sweet but somehow not enough to fill the void left by Mork.

A couple of years passed and we started to get the feeling that we needed to get a small companion dog. We spent months researching the breeds of dogs that would fit with our needs, and we were about settled on either a Pug or a Boston Terrier. While driving one day, we passed a pet store and saw a sign outside that said, 'Puggleys'. 'Puggley? What is a Puggley?' we asked each other. So we turned the car around and went back to find out what a Puggley was.

We went in and saw a little fellow in a cage. He looked a little like a tiny brown bear. I was in love at first sight. This was a pet shop where I had stopped many, many times over the years to look at the pups. I was never tempted to buy before. I would never have considered buying a dog from a pet shop like this, which might for all I knew be getting pups from a puppy mill. We went home without the little brown bear-doggy but he was on my mind the whole night. I insisted we go back and see if he was still there the next day. By morning light I was determined that the little fellow would be mine.

I brought him home and sent out an announcement that we had a new family member and I included a photo. Several people asked, 'What is it?' I looked at the photo and had to admit he was a nondescript sort of creature. I realized that in the photo he looked very much like a kitten. I had to send a disclaimer explaining that we had gotten a pup. We named him Zammis. He immediately bonded with me and very soon had me running him to the vet with an emergency – just like old times. I began to notice that Zammis' mannerisms resembled Mork's. He would sit with his back to me just like Mork did, like he was guarding me. The colour of his fur (the undercoat) was similar to the colour of Mork's fur. Mork had been perhaps part Maine Coon and he had a bit of a mane around his head and neck, and so did Zammis. And then there were the corn chips. Mork had been a fanatic for corn tortilla chips. If I was eating them he would jump up in my lap and snatch them right from my hand as I was about to put them in my mouth. Zammis began doing the same thing. Zammis is always on the spot as soon as he hears me munching on corn chips and insists on getting a chip in very much the same way Mork did. Zammis seems to have many cat-like traits. He also had a sweet relationship with Korkey who was here as Mork grew old. Korkey welcomed Zammis without any cat vs dog conflict. I used to catch them relaxing on the bed, with Korkey stretching out, reaching paw to paw as if she recognized that Zammis was a cat, too.

I now have seven dogs and I have had many cats over the years, but my relationship with Mork was so different and so special, and my relationship with Zammis feels so much the same. I do feel a special soul connection with them. I can't say for sure that they are the same soul, but I have a strong feeling that Mork is with me still and always will be.

IF THEY COULD TALK
Charlotte sent me this story.

I lost my little parrot, Messinah, just before Christmas last year. She was like my own baby for the year and a half we spent together. I was completely gutted when she died in my arms. When I bought my next baby Kakariki (which is what she was), Kizzie, I noticed that she'd been born exactly two months to the day after my Messinah died. And she is so much like her it is uncanny, in her behaviour and her attitude toward me. She got on Messinah's cremation box the other day and just stared at the photo I have behind it of me and Messinah. Also on the one-month anniversary of Messinah's death, when I was crying about her, I suddenly noticed one of her yellow feathers poking out of my trouser pocket, which was spooky because I didn't own those trousers when I had her and I know for a fact my pockets had been empty. I think it was a wing feather. Of course I kept it and, like I say, a month later Kizzie was born!

One more thing: Messinah had an accident when she was about six months old whereby she caught her head in the door just as it was being closed, and forever after that her right eye always looked as if she was squinting where she had damaged it, although her left eye was perfectly normal. And it's exactly the same with Kizzie, though of course she hasn't had any accidents. She just always looks as if she's squinting. The vet said there was nothing wrong with her when I took her to see him.

It's great when people get some physical evidence of their pet's return, as it is so compelling.

THE CHANGELING

Jan wrote to tell me this.

Several years ago I was sitting in the lounge one night surrounded by my crystals, which I was sorting out, with my Egyptian Mau cat, Simba, sitting in front of me, watching. I looked up from what I was doing and we both looked at each other, and then something unbelievable happened. I saw Simba's face and body change slowly into a completely different cat. His whole face and body changed and he was much, much thinner in shape, along with having a completely different coloured coat!

I knew straight away he was my cat from a past life. Then his features turned back to Simba's and he just smiled at me! It was an amazing moment and one I will never forget.

GOLDEN EYES
This is Judy's story.

Losing my beautiful cat, about 12 years ago, made me feel like never having another one because I'd loved the one I lost so much. But just over two years ago I decided that I needed to have cats in my life again. I wanted two cats this time so that they could keep each other company. At that time my daughter's cat had three kittens, one boy, one girl and another one that couldn't be determined, so we all decided it was a girl. I wanted two girls because my old cat had been a male and I didn't want to betray him by having the same sex again. It would have seemed like I was trying to replace him. So when they were six weeks old, I took the two female kittens home and left my daughter with the one boy. My two little girls were very different: one was a short-haired, black-and-white kitten I named Candy, and the other was a long-haired black Persian-looking girl I named Cleo. I loved them both dearly and they were the greatest of friends, till they got to about six months old, when my 'Cleo' turned into a 'Leo'. He'd got much bigger than his sister and then his male anatomy appeared. I now know he did this to shield the fact he actually was a boy because he knew I wanted two girls and I wouldn't have taken him if I'd known he was a boy.

He got bigger and bigger and was also a big bully to his sister. That got worse over time, and I always had to watch him when she was around. It also became apparent that he was possessive of me, as he followed me everywhere, and that became a problem. He just wanted me to himself and didn't want to share me with his sister.

Leo had always had a breathing problem since he was born. He was never able to meow or purr and he coughed a lot. This was due to a valve in his throat not opening and closing properly. The vet told me that they could do an operation for his problem, but it didn't always work and could cause other problems. So, as Leo managed very well, I left it. He did not need to 'talk', as I always knew what he wanted and needed. He had the most beautiful, enormous golden eyes and he always knew how to communicate through them.

Leo died just two months ago, at the very young age of two years and four months, peacefully and naturally, on our driveway. It was, and still is, a traumatic time for me, as I miss him so much. I knew he wouldn't live a long life, but never thought he'd go quite so young. Since his passing I've come to believe that he might have been a reincarnation of the beloved cat we had years before because he certainly shared a lot of traits with him. I feel that his purpose on this Earth this time round was to bring unconditional love back to me, and he certainly did that very well.

The clincher for me was when I had a spiritual drawing done of Leo, which sits up proud and high in my crystal healing room. The drawing is very accurate of him as an adult cat, and his eyes dominate the picture, just as they did in real life. But you see, the only photo I had taken of him was when 'he' (I thought he was a 'she' then) was only eight weeks old, and the artist never saw it, so to have this A3 portrait of him is quite something. I had only had a spiritual message telling me to take a photo of my cats the week before he died, and I said to myself, 'Oh yes, I must do that sometime.' If only I had listened to my inner self. Never mind, this is a wonderful portrait and I am forever grateful to the woman who did it. It is done in pastel and, as he was a big black cat, there is much black in it and these wonderful huge golden eyes.

FROM A CAT TO A KING

Patsy's story tells us about a message from a beloved cat.

My cat, Sassy, always reminded me of a lion. When I first got her as a little fluffy kitten, she was a gorgeous tawny colour. Her coat was very short and smooth, and people always thought she looked like a small lioness. She grew up into a cat who retained her playfulness, and every birthday I'd buy her a new toy to play with. She was a bit odd because she never chased birds. I found that strange. She'd sit and watch them, but it was as if they were beneath her somehow. She was my best mate for many years, and I always felt that maybe we'd known each other before. When she got ill, aged 17, I was devastated. I knew she was going to die because she kept saying goodbye in various ways. For instance, even though she was weak, she brought all her toys to me and laid them in a pile by my chair. I held her in my arms when the vet administered his merciful injection, and my heart broke as she went limp. Once she'd gone, the house seemed so empty. Seventeen years is a long time.

I missed her constantly and so wanted some sort of sign from her, but got nothing. It was a really bad time for me. One day I felt like I couldn't take it any more, and when I left the house that day to drive to work I told her in my mind, 'Sassy, you have to give me a sign. If you can still hear me, if you're still somewhere, then show me a new cat that I can't miss on my way to work.' I lived in the countryside, and there were only two cats in the village. So seeing a cat was quite rare and seeing a different one, next to impossible. As I drove I scanned the hedgerows looking for something, but there wasn't anything. As I turned the final bend into the town I couldn't believe my eyes: a circus was coming to town, and right there on the verge was a huge billboard – and on it a roaring lion. At first I was shocked and delighted, thinking this at last was my sign, but then logic stepped in and I started to doubt – after all, I knew Sassy *looked* like a lion, but she wasn't one, and the poster must have been put there the previous night, before I'd asked for a sign. I know they say a healthy mind will always look for the logical answer, but this time I wished mine wouldn't! Why couldn't I just believe?

I decided to take further action. I thought I'd go and see a medium, and if she mentioned the lion poster without me telling her about it, then it had to be a real sign from Sassy. I went and, although the reading was good, the medium never mentioned the poster. It was frustrating. In the end I asked her outright: was there a cat trying to get through to me? Her answer left me speechless. She said, 'Not a cat as such, not a domestic one anyway.

I'm quite sure there's a mistake here somewhere, but you didn't ever own a lion, did you?' She went on, 'Ah, I see, this is a message from what was a cat. She wants you to know that she's now returned to her true form, what she was in previous lives. Your cat is now a lion again.'

THE DONKEY WHO THOUGHT SHE WAS A HORSE

Carrie sent me this story.

It was five years ago when Mildred the donkey came into my life. For years I'd had horses, but at this point I'd gotten too old to cope with another, whether it had been a youngster that needed a firm hand, or an older pre-owned horse, which usually came with some issue or other. Besides, I'd decided to sell most of the land as I'd tired of its constant upkeep, and the two acres I was keeping wasn't enough for a horse. So, a friend talked me into getting a donkey and a couple of sheep to keep the grass nice. Donkeys don't wear shoes and don't run about so much as horses, who would have churned the mud up in the winter. Plus, as my friend said, there were lots of donkeys needing homes, and we had a sanctuary on the doorstep. I discovered she was right and I fell in love with a pretty little jenny, all soft grey fur and ridiculous ears.

I took her home and she settled down happily with two Hebridean sheep I also took in.

It was a few weeks later that I started to notice some odd behaviour in the jenny, who was called Mildred. She started to work herself in circles. She would canter first one way and then the other, going back to trot in the middle crossover place, so that she was always on the right leg. (I should explain here for the non-horsey that, for horses, the canter is a three-way gait, and to be in perfect balance they need to 'lead' off on the correct foreleg – the right for a right circle and the left for a left circle.) Every day Mildred would work for half an hour, all by herself, with just the sheep watching her bemusedly. Of course I watched her, too. After about a week of practice she mastered the 'flying change' and no longer had to drop back to trot to change her lead leg. It was amazing! The first day she did it she came over to me where I stood watching and snorted as if to say, 'See, I did it!' And just like that, as she gazed into my eyes, my mind went back about 50 years to another set of eyes that used to stare into mine. I'd once owned a big grey mare that I'd loved to distraction. I'd got her when she was 16 years old and she'd not been well brought up. Still, there was something about her that I really loved. Charisma had been her name, and that was what she'd had, in spades. I'd wanted to do dressage with her and she had wonderful, natural paces. She was the most well-balanced horse I ever had. Too well-balanced, in fact, because it meant that she didn't feel any need to change lead legs in canter. I was never successful in teaching her to do a flying change — she just didn't see the need. And so, although she competed on a novice level with me and we enjoyed it, I could never progress her to intermediate or advanced because I could never rely on her to do a flying change. I lost Charisma to colic when she was 22, and I never thought I'd ever get over it. All this came back to mind as I stood there that day, and I swear that when I came back to Earth, that donkey was smiling at me. Was Mildred my horse Charisma come back to me to do that one thing for me? I'll never know for sure, but from that day Mildred never did another 'horsey' thing, so I know what I believe.

I'd be interested to see any animal behaviourists find a logical explanation for this one. I loved this story partly because I love horses so much, but I think it also shows that not only do animals have souls, they also have a sense of humour!

CHAPTER 5

Animal Angels

Pets who have been infused with the spark of an angel, sometimes for a moment and sometimes for a whole lifetime

Angels come in many shapes and forms, including that of fur and feather.

– JENNY SMEDLEY

AN ANGEL CHOIR FOR GOLDIE

Fausteen told me this lovely story.

Before our daughter was born, my husband came home one day with two ginger kittens, and they were delightful.

We named them Brownie and Goldie after the colour of the collars they wore. When they were about 18 months old, Brownie went missing. I received a call at work – a kind stranger (or angel, maybe?) told me he had removed Brownie's collar from the corpse he'd found on the roadside and was thus able to pass on this sad news.

That evening, Goldie and I were in the kitchen, both looking toward the window. Goldie let out a grief-stricken sound I had never heard before or since and turned his head to me with an expression of profound sadness.

Goldie remained with us for another ten years until, finally, he got sick. He spent a night at the vet's but, knowing he was dying, I brought him home. He painfully made his way upstairs, calling out to our daughter and, not finding her in her room, settling down in the passage to wait. When our daughter returned with her dad, Goldie was what I call 'travelling': his breathing had the death rattle and he could barely move. We were having our bedroom re-modelled at that time and were sleeping in the lounge, but I remained with Goldie and our daughter in her room until the small hours. Eventually, I crept downstairs.

Some while later I awoke to the sound of music – beautiful, indescribable music. Startled, I thought it was the radio alarm clock above in our bedroom, and I roused my husband and asked that he go check. He reported that the radio alarm was unplugged. However, he also discovered that Goldie had passed. The music I heard? It was the Heavenly Host greeting our much, much loved pet home.

Angels will use all and any means to bring us messages from our loved ones. Music is one method I've heard about many times.

Genevieve Frederick is the Executive Director/Founder of an organization that feeds the pets of the homeless in the USA. If any pets can be said to embody angelic qualities, then it's some of those that her charity helps. These pets make life bearable for those who have nothing and give them something to cling to in their desperate lives. They bring love to the unloved. Genevieve was able to share some stories from the people who help the homeless and the pets for whom they care. Divine intervention certainly seems to play a role in these stories.

THE BEST OF FRIENDS

Last Saturday I forgot to bring the donated pet food inside from the van. Since I was tired and it was late, I left it until morning and completely forgot about it until leaving for church on Sunday morning. I didn't have time to unload it and left to pick up my two granddaughters. As we dashed off on the freeway, I missed my turn, which meant two miles to the next exit. When we arrived at the intersection where we were going to turn around, the light was red. While I waited I glanced to my left, biding my time until the light turned green. There was a homeless man with two big Labradors by his side. I rolled my window down and asked if he needed food for the dogs. I heard a quick, 'Yes!' and I gave him several bags. When he told me he had a third dog that wasn't with him, I added another bag. Smiling, he said, 'God bless you!' and 'Thank you.' With tails wagging, the dogs walked eagerly around the bags, sniffing and hoping for a treat. The man never asked for a handout or anything for himself. This was a true need and I was grateful I'd left the dog food overnight in the van.

I gave the man information on where he could get more dog food (*The Bridge*, downtown Dallas, at the Homeless Shelter) and again, he expressed his gratitude, still not asking anything for himself.

One never knows when the opportunity will come to serve the pets of the homeless. I don't feel this is a coincidence, rather that I was guided to someone who really needed help. Thanks for giving Dallas the opportunity to help those in similar circumstances.

LOVE ME, LOVE MY DOG

This story comes from a formerly homeless person.

I myself was one of those people. Until recently I was homeless and living out of my car. My boyfriend and I usually slept on the couch at various different acquaintances' and relatives' houses when we could not afford a motel room. Then about six years ago I walked into a house that belonged to the friend of a friend. The man who lived there was supposed to be taking care of our mutual friend's dog, but when I walked in the door I saw the dog was covered in cuts and gashes (many were still open and bleeding) and I asked what had happened to the dog. His reply was, 'I beat her ass with the weed-whacker.' He snickered to himself with amusement when he told me this, and he pointed to the corner of the room where I saw a weed-eater with blood and clumps of fur on it. So I immediately removed the dog from the situation. I did not have anywhere of my own to call home at the time, much less anywhere I could go with the dog. So from that night on I slept in the car with the dog while my boyfriend slept in the house on the couch of whatever person's home we were staying at on any given night. My dog and I lived in the car through winters and summers and everything in between for almost five years because I did not have anywhere to go where I could have my dog, too. About a year ago, however, my parents asked me to move back into their house because they didn't like me sleeping in my car somewhere. And they agreed to let me keep my dog at their house, too, since they know that if the dog doesn't come with then I am not going to go. I hope that good luck like mine will find the many homeless and their pets, too.

KEEPING PERFECT PACE

In the pecking order of man and beast, there was no lower rung than the one shared by Randy Vargas and Foxy on the streets of Hoboken. He was 46 and homeless, regular work – like his fondly remembered machine-shop job – long in the past. Foxy was a member of dogdom's least-fashionable demographic: a ten-year-old brindled Pit Bull, compact as a pick-up truck, ears askew, two-tone face, white neck and the rest an arbitrary mix of light and dark.

And yet in this city increasingly defined by creatures who drew the long straw – winners in property and on Wall Street, sleek Goldens, pampered Yorkies, fashionable Puggles and Doodles – there was something transcendent in their bond. Maybe in a world of opaque relationships, theirs was a lesson in charity like a parable from the Bible.

He had rescued her back when she was homeless and abused, a scared runty thing living with homeless men who had no use for her. She in turn gave him purpose, companionship and love.

Maybe it was how the relationship brought out the best in both. It brought Randy to life and into the world, as much a part of Hoboken street life as any young comer with his black Lab. And it made Foxy a creature of eternal sweetness, unfailingly friendly to people and animals, tail-wagging at the merest glance, a Pit Bull in name but not spirit.

So if you spent any time in Hoboken, the odds are pretty good you would have seen the two of them, sleeping in front of the Saints Peter and Paul Parish Center, visiting the Hoboken Animal Hospital, walking down the street – Foxy keeping perfect pace with Randy, dressed in winter in raffish layers of sweatshirts and T-shirts plucked from the St Mary's Hospital Thrift Store.

Cheryl remembered seeing Mr Vargas resting on a condo's shaded concrete steps on a sweltering August weekend day, flat on his back with Foxy in the same position one step below. It was the perfect image of man and dog, she said, and added, 'This really was a dog with a deep soul.' Everyone who knew them said the same thing: Mr Vargas cared for the dog better than for himself. If it was the dead of winter, the dog would get all the blankets and he'd get the pavement with nothing on it, said a groomer at the Hoboken Animal Hospital. 'If it was raining, he'd put the umbrella up for the dog before he'd put it up for himself.'

But there's not much margin for error at the bottom rung. Once this winter he was arrested, accused of making threatening remarks to women. The case was dismissed, and friends say it should never have gone that far. But Ms Murphy had to rescue Foxy from the pound in Newark, where she could have been euthanized.

It all ended so fast, people still can't explain it. Aside from a dog run, Foxy had seldom been seen off the leash, but on the morning of 19 March in the park, she was. She saw a dog she knew across Hudson Street, dashed across to say hello and was hit by a white pick-up which stopped briefly and then sped off. Mr Vargas held the dog, blood spurting from her mouth, and waved at passing cars, but none stopped. So he carried her 60 pounds, feeling the broken bones in his hand, as far as he could, then put her down and ran to the Animal Hospital for help. But it was too late.

People come by the Animal Hospital every day, some fighting back tears, to leave donations – more than $900 so far. Some come from people who knew them, most from people who feel like they did. Alone they might have been invisible. Together, they're still around. Her picture is in some store windows, wearing a gray sweatshirt with a red T-shirt under it, gazing to the right like a sentry, a wondrous study in essence of dog with a touch of human thrown in.

In different ways, they're still around. Her picture is in some store windows, wearing a gray sweatshirt with a red T-shirt under it, gazing to the right like a sentry, a wondrous study in essence of dog with a touch of human thrown in.

Since the accident Mr Vargas has had good days and bad ones, sometimes being up and around, sometimes, like the other day, looking groggy and defeated under his red comforter on the street. 'I feel,' he told a friend, 'like I have a hole in my soul.'

At the Animal Hospital they're buying a pendant to hold some of Foxy's ashes which he can wear around his neck. Friends check on him regularly, bring him food, talk of finally getting him a place to live. There's talk of getting him a new dog when he's ready, which surely isn't now.

'It's like most relationships,' Mr Vargas says from under the red blanket. 'You have to wait for the right time.'

THE TWO OF US

Many years ago I lived on the streets. I had a pet hooded rat, my first rat. His name was Benjamin. I am sure, looking back now, that what I fed him was not what a healthy rat needed to eat. But he never went hungry. He and I shared everything we found to eat. His home was a cardboard box and he lived in it happily. He never tried to run away, amazingly. When I slept in the parks or on the waterfront, Ben would curl up in my jacket. Sometimes in the middle of the night when it got extra spooky, just the feeling of Ben's little body pressed next to mine kept me sane. When Ben got too old to continue living on the streets, the founder of the Mustard Seed [a home caring for the most vulnerable] took him in. He moved into a huge aquarium (must have been a 50 gallon, or at least to my little eyes it seemed that big) and had every luxury a rat could want. After he went to live there the streets got a tad scarier. I actually still get tears in my eyes when I remember Ben; he was awesome.

It gives me faith in human nature when I read that there are people like Genevieve caring for the homeless and their angelic pets.

HAVE A BREAK!
Gemma told me this story.

My cat, Kitkat, is like a guardian angel to my daughter. We got Kitkat as a kitten, when my daughter was just a baby, and she hasn't left her side since. If Kitkat sees Hannah doing something dangerous, like trying to touch the fire or cooker, or if Hannah falls over, Kitkat will meow and meow until Hannah stops what she was doing, or until I or my partner come and help. If Hannah cries, Kitkat will jump up next to her and lick her like she's one of her babies, until she stops crying. She doesn't act like a cat at all; for instance if my hamsters escape, she'll pick them up very gently and bring them to me or my partner, and she doesn't hurt them. It's as if she knows they're family and shouldn't be out, and she watches until I put them back in their cage where they should be.

Stephanie tells this story about a sprightly Springer Spaniel.

THE INTUITIVE DOG

In July 2007 my brother gave a Springer Spaniel pup to my daughters Sarah and Ciara. The excitement of choosing a name began, and we finally decided on Sparkle, and she's lived up to it ever since. From the moment she arrived she was full of fun and has brought us a huge amount of pleasure. When I meditated, she would whine outside the door until allowed in to join me, and through this we've bonded very closely.

I became ill the following year, and Sparkle would lie on me and follow me about in a very protective way. She's very intuitive and took every opportunity to comfort me. With my daughters in school and my husband at work, this canine company, I believe, helped me through a tough time with the unconditional loving way she cared for me.

I believe she was sent to help us all through this. We've since also rescued a Husky mix pup from an animal rescue centre and called her Crystal. Both dogs are highly intuitive and sensitive to our energies. We're so lucky and blessed to have them.

I've just read an amazing story in the newspapers. This was about a retired headmaster called John Lawes. Mr Lawes used to walk the dog regularly (unfortunately the paper neglected to name the dog or its breeding, which is sadly indicative of the journalist's attitude to the importance of pets!). Apparently one evening Mr Lawes' wife noticed the dog behaving strangely; it kept sitting and staring at her husband in what she described as 'a quizzical fashion'. It was so unusual that she asked her husband if anything odd had happened. Mr Lawes then confessed that during the walk that day he'd got his feet entangled in the dog's lead and fallen quite heavily. He said he'd banged his head, but only on a soft piece of ground, and that he was fine. Mrs Lawes retired to bed and it was only later that she heard a shout from her husband. She hurried downstairs to find him collapsed on the floor. Knowing that he'd had a fall, she immediately called an ambulance. Sadly it was to no avail, as Mr Lawes had suffered a terminal brain haemorrhage. He died. Mrs Lawes was left to puzzle over the fact that their dog had tried to tell them something was wrong despite the outward appearance of normality.

CHRISTMAS MAGIC

Kathleen told me this lovely story.

Alfie was a lovely ginger-and-white fluff ball when we got him as a kitten and grew into a very beautiful boy. He had a tail like Basil Brush and a beautiful mane on his chest, which made him look like a lion. He was a nervous but very affectionate wee thing. He loved to chase pigeons around the garden, although never once caught one. We all loved him so dearly; he really was part of the family and would wait for us to return at the top of the stairs, although sometimes he'd be asleep and the moment he heard the door open you'd hear the thud as he jumped down onto the floor to come greet us. Alfie only ever got sick once — in fact it was two months before he passed at just three years old. He picked up a virus which we got treated straight away and within 24 hours he was right as rain. Luckily, my daughter came home for two days from university as, unbeknownst to us this would be the last time she would see dear Alfie. We were sitting watching TV when he suddenly jumped up and sat looking around the room, staring up at the ceiling like something was there and then seeming rather frightened. Jokingly my youngest made a comment, 'He must have seen a ghost!'

The following day my daughter gave her usual cuddles and goodbyes, which always held my husband up as he sat waiting in the car. The following day Alfie woke me up as he would always do, standing on two legs, meowing at me at the side of my pillow, like he was talking to me. I got up and let him out. It was a beautiful summer's morning. I sat watching him pacing up and down, chasing butterflies and pigeons. He'd sit under his favourite rose bush, waiting. I watched him launch himself and scratch the fence as he tried with all his efforts to catch a pigeon.

I went upstairs and got ready and my husband brought Alfie in and fed him, and then my son and husband got into the car and waited for me to come down. Suddenly I noticed Alfie coming up the stairs, but not in his usual manner. He looked frightened and he turned to come to me and suddenly rolled over. I ran over to him, realizing something wasn't right. I thought he was having a fit, as he loved to catch bees. Just as I was about to go down the stairs to get help, I heard him take a breath (unknown to me, it was his last breath). I remember touching his cheek, just under his eye, and telling him how much I loved him. I ran downstairs and my husband came up to see what had happened. We were afraid to touch Alfie in case he was fitting. I knew he'd passed but I refused to accept it. My husband picked him up and he just gave me that look. I knew Alfie'd gone and I went to pieces.

We took Alfie's body to the vet, who confirmed it was more than likely a heart attack. We said our goodbyes and I told him how much we loved him, and to go into the light where the family would be waiting for him. It broke our hearts. Over that first week when I was sitting alone, twice I could have sworn he was at the side of me meow-ing. I thought I'd imagined it the first time, but the second time I heard the sound he'd make when he yawned.

A few weeks later we were packing to go off to Cornwall. My son started yelling at us to come outside. A pigeon had been sitting under the windowsill. Then it walked into our hallway and into the kitchen, turned around and walked into the lounge, whereupon my hus-band let it out the patio door. I think that it was Alfie's way of letting us know he was there, because he loved pigeons so much.

Recently I was at the garden centre and the Christmas decorations were all going up. There was a sale area with a Christmas cat bauble and a wind-up musical merry-go-round. I wound it up and I was gobsmacked when it played 'You are my sunshine' because that was the song I sang to Alfie the day his ashes came home.

I agree with Kathleen that this was a sign from Alfie. After all, a song about sunshine isn't really what you'd expect a Christmas decoration to play, is it?

ANGELS WITH WINGS
This is Maggie's story.

Smudge was a canary rather than a cat or dog as you might have expected. He used to live with his mate Sam, until Sam had a stroke, and despite the vet's best efforts his condition worsened, so with tears in my eyes I had to have the bird put to sleep. I'd heard of the Rainbow Bridge, where our pets go to until it's our turn to go to the other side, but had no idea how fast the transition was.

Within days Smudge was reacting to an unseen presence, getting agitated and staring at the ceiling, until I took a digipic and there in the photo was a faint orb over the cage. I believe Sam visits regularly to see how Smudge is getting on, and as a psychic person I just sense the bird in the room, sometimes briefly. Then one day the flash wouldn't go off despite new batteries being put in and the result was a blue light in the room that was almost ultraviolet, which canaries and budgies can see, hence Smudge I think was finally able to see Sam. After that Smudge was content and the camera resumed normal operation.

CHAPTER 6

Magical Healers

Pets who have healed their owners or helped their owners heal other people

Some pets know exactly whom they're meant to be with and will go to great lengths to be where they're destined to be.

– JENNY SMEDLEY

NURSE CASSIE

Jo sent me this story.

My dog Cassie is a Staffy cross English Bull Terrier, and we adopted her from Dogs Trust Roden [Shropshire] in

November 2009. I have clinical depression, but a lot of the time I am OK, and after years of having it I've learned to 'put on a front'. However, Cassie always knows when I'm feeling low, and instead of being her usual bouncy, clumsy self, will approach me very calmly and tenderly. And instead of walking on top of me like she usually will, she'll sit next to me and just rest her head on my lap.

She is a lot like my old dog Jess, who we had from when I was 11 until I was 22. I was bullied at school, and Jess was also from the Dogs Trust. When I'd get in from school after a bad day, I'd shut myself in my bedroom and have a cry (trying to be as quiet as possible so my brothers didn't hear!). But after a minute or so I'd hear scratching at the door, and it would be Jess. She would always come in to comfort me and look after me. Sometimes I feel that Cassie is a reincarnation of Jessy. They both have the same beautiful brown eyes, and although their personalities are quite different (Jess was very timid and Cassie is very confident!), I feel that deep soul connection with both of them. Even when I'm thinking about something, it's as if Cassie knows what I'm thinking. I'll be walking her and thinking, 'Cassie, if you need to poo, please poo here! The next dog poo bin isn't for ages!' And then she'll look at me and well, you know, do her business!

ANGEL WINGS

Hailie shared this story with me.

I had a very close bond with my rabbit Tyler. He came to me at a very low time in my life and helped me through it with his love and affection, and he made me realize that the world was not such a bad place and showed me what true love was. Sadly, two and a half years after I got him, he passed away, which devastated me. Looking back I wonder whether he was sent to heal me, and once his job was done he had to leave, as by the time he passed I was settled in a relationship and had my son and was pregnant with my daughter. Tyler also had markings on his nose which resembled angel's wings, which could be purely coincidental but he helped me in so many ways that, to me, he will always be my guardian angel.

EARTH ANGEL

While we're on the subject of angels, here's Monika's story.

Yesterday my 'Angel on Earth', Wilma, went to the Rainbow Bridge. She really was my angel on Earth. She came to me almost 11 years ago at the age of one and a half. I rescued her from some people who didn't want her anymore. Their loss was my gain. They never realized what they had. Since the first moment we met, she gave me everything. She never was mine, she loved everyone, but most of all she gave me the will to go forward through all the hard times I've had. She accepted me the way I am, and with her I never had to be an actor. This was very important to me because I never used to get along very well with humans, and I always had problems with them. My whole life has been a problem. Every time I think things are going good, they go wrong again. I have two other dogs, but they are not Wilma. I love them, but it's not the same. Right now I feel lonely and sad and I don't know how to go forward without my angel on Earth.

Monika's story made me feel very sad, but because Wilma obviously came along specifically to help and heal her, I feel she will undoubtedly be back because the job isn't finished.

COME OUTSIDE!

Josie's story is an inspiring one (Josie's name has been changed, as she now has a very responsible job she doesn't want to jeopardize).

I developed agoraphobia when I was in my thirties. I'd had a daughter and the doctors said I was suffering from postnatal depression. But it got worse. First I didn't want to take Charity, my baby girl, out in her buggy. My hubby, Dave, bought me a big old-fashioned carriage pram because he thought maybe I felt Charity was too vulnerable in the little buggy. At first that did help, but gradually I started making excuses not to go out: it was too cold, too hot, too windy, there wasn't time, I had to wait in for a delivery, etc. Soon we were only going out in the car. It took months, but eventually I had to ask Dave to leave the car in the garage until I'd got inside it. Then we couldn't go out at all after dark. Then he'd have to drop me off right outside whatever shop I wanted to go in and pick me up the same way when I'd finished. Soon I was having all the groceries delivered and doing any other shopping online.

I had always intended to go back to work, and I really wanted to, but there was no chance of that. It finally was at its peak when I started rearranging the furniture so that I didn't have to walk through the middle of the room. Dave was patient, but he started cursing the fact that all the rooms were getting harder to get into. There was always something half-blocking the way. I thought he was going to have me sectioned or something, but he didn't; he did something else: he brought me home a dog. It turned out that a mate at work had been desperate to re-home his dog. It was a Shetland Sheepdog called Jay, and the mate's wife had got sick of dog hairs everywhere and having to keep grooming him. I'd always loved dogs, but I couldn't believe Dave's timing! I couldn't take our daughter for a walk, so how could I walk a dog? I couldn't even stand at the open door, so how could I let Jay out into the garden? Still, I loved that dog. I loved grooming him while Charity was asleep; somehow it soothed me. I didn't think of anything while I was brushing his silky coat. But of course he had to wait until evening, when Dave got in, to go for a walk. I got around to letting him out to do his business by using only the front garden. We had a small porch that had its door on the side, so I was able to open that because I wasn't facing the road. I don't know why that worked, but it did. I'd just open the door enough for Jay to get through, shut it quickly and then watch through the glass until he wanted to come back in, then do the same in reverse. This worked for a while, but Jay seemed to want me to go out there with him, and I just couldn't. Life was bad because I was so limited, and Jay would sit, his head on my knee, regarding me solemnly as if trying to figure out how to help me.

Dave had always made the postman swear to shut the garden gate behind him, and he always did. Tradesmen I would tell as they were leaving to shut the gate, and they did. But one day, in late spring, we had a relief postman, and I didn't see until it was too late that he'd left the gate swinging. Jay went down the path straight to the open gate. I called him and, although he looked back, he took slow steps forwards as if daring me to come get him. By the time he was on the pavement I was hoarse with yelling, and Charity had woken up and joined in with her bawling. Still Jay kept going. He walked two or three steps onto the road, glancing back to see what I was doing. Along the road, to my horror, I could see an oil tanker approaching. Jay had moved to stand between two parked cars. He took one look back at me and I understood: if I didn't go out there and get him, he was going to walk into the path of the tanker, which by then would have had no chance of stopping. That did it. I unfroze my feet and ran up the garden path. As I got near to Jay I saw his mouth open in a triumphant grin. I grabbed his collar and the tanker swept past, bathing us in a shower of dust and displaced air.

That afternoon I put Charity in her pram and, on shaking legs, pushed it, with Jay attached by his lead to the handle, down to the park, around the park and back home. I even picked a few daffodils (which was banned!) to show Dave, or I feared he would never believe me.

Josie tells me that the following year she was head-hunted for a really great job, and everything fell into place for her.

She found a great childcare facility and, just when she was wondering what she could do about Jay being cared for, she met a woman suffering from bulimia who was at her wits' end. When Josie asked if she'd care to have the company of an amazing dog during the day, the woman was very happy to say yes. Josie had a feeling Jay would work his magic on her. I'll let you know if she was right in my next book.

LESSONS FROM TYSON

Simon, a success coach in Australia, sent me this story which had me in tears, but it's such a beautiful story that I hope you'll forgive me if it has you, too, reaching for the tissues. At the end, though, there is a follow-up from me that might make you smile again. If you'd like to connect with Simon, his website details are in the Resources chapter at the back of the book.

As a writer and a success coach, I've spent much of my life studying what makes us humans do what we do, how we interact with each other and, above all, what makes us happy – or not. I've dedicated my time, my energy and my passion, not to making money and accumulating material possessions, but to learning how to inspire people – including myself – to be as happy as possible.

On this journey I've been fortunate to have had many wise and compassionate teachers, including some of the world's top personal growth experts, and yet in all this time, my most insightful, wise, gentle and caring teacher was not a 'guru' or an expert, or even a human being. He was my faithful and utterly adorable darling dog, Tyson.

Before I met Tyson, I already wanted to be a success coach, but I had a wound deep in my heart that stemmed from not fully loving myself which prevented me from being truly successful, just as it does for millions of others. Now, thanks to Tyson, I am a success coach, my wound is healed and I'm living my dream life helping others heal theirs. And all because one kind-hearted dog was able to do what no one else ever could: he taught me how to love myself!

Tyson came into my life in the most remarkable way nine years ago, at a time when I had lost my way professionally, my relationship was on unsteady ground and, worst of all, I was suffering from a self-imposed sense of isolation brought about by the growing realization that, although I had many friends, I'd never met anyone in all my years – and all my travels – who was like me. I kept thinking that one day I would. But after 42 years, 'one day' had never come. I felt like a misfit, an aberration, an alien in a foreign world. I mean, I had two eyes, two ears and a nose. But the thoughts in my head and the feelings in my heart seemed to be different to everyone else's. I seemed to feel emotions more acutely than others. For a grown man, I wept a lot – mainly at the images of suffering on the nightly news. Stories about war or hunger or – worst of all – animal cruelty pierced my heart as though it were me who was experiencing them.

I yearned to give love unconditionally, and yet I didn't know how. So I shrank back into myself and slipped deeper and deeper into depression.

Then one day I received a phone call from a close friend of mine called Nicole. She knew I was struggling, and she knew that my beautiful and loving partner at the time, Dana, was also struggling. So she suggested we might like to look after a dog for some friends of hers who were returning to England and needed someone to mind him for six months before sending him on to join them. The way rabies quarantine laws work in the UK is that if you live abroad and you want to bring your dog into the country, you have two choices: you can either bring them with you and put them in a cage in some ghastly quarantine facility for six months, or choose the much kinder option of giving them an anti-rabies shot and leaving them with a foster family, who after six months can then put them on a plane to the UK where they will be cleared to go straight home to you. So that was the deal.

Look after the dog – whom Nicole described as being the size of a small lion – for six months and then put him on a plane to England.

I declined Nicole's offer, partly because I felt at the time that having a large dog to look after would be a burden, and also because we only had a small garden and I felt it would be unfair to him. I'd never had a dog before. When I was young my father had a black Labrador called Bess and I loved her with all my heart, but I was still a child when she died and I felt I might not have what it took to look after a dog properly. Nicole pushed the issue. She knew that her friends were starting to panic because they were due to fly out in a few weeks and they hadn't yet found someone to take care of their dog – which, after further questioning, I discovered was a very large four-year-old Rottweiler–German Shepherd cross called Tyson. Now, if I asked you to picture a huge dog that was half Rottweiler and half German Shepherd, and weighed 50kg, the image that would spring into your mind is probably much the same as the one that sprang into mine! I pictured the kind of intimidating attack dogs the Nazis used to patrol the perimeters of their evil concentration camps, all muscles, teeth and salivating jaws powerful enough to bite your leg clean off! I refused politely. Nicole sounded sad but said she understood, and I thought that was that.

Then the following week she called again.

'Are you sure?' she said. 'I think a dog would be so good for you. Why don't you just go and meet him?' It was now just two weeks before Chloe and Paul, Tyson's owners, were due to fly and they still hadn't found any-one willing to take care of him. It was looking as though they would have to put him in a cage for six months, and they were clearly distraught. 'He's a beautiful dog, not at all like you imagine,' Nicole went on. 'I know you'll fall in love with him and I just feel, I don't know... like you're meant to be together.'

But my mind was made up.

A few days later she rang yet again. 'Something is tell-ing me you should be the one to care for Tyson,' she said. 'I don't know why; I just have a feeling about it.'

Looking back now, I can't recall if I was swayed by what she said. All I know is that I rejected her a third time and that when I hung up the phone I felt how Jesus' disciple, Peter, must have felt after his third denial ... as though I had just done something very wrong, although I didn't know what.

The following Wednesday – four days before Chloe and Peter were going to put Tyson in a cage and board their flight back to the UK without him – I found myself waiting outside a motorcycle repair shop 30km away on the other side of town while the mechanics gave my beloved Kawasaki its annual service. My mobile phone rang. It was Nicole.

'I know you don't want him,' she said immediately. 'But I thought I'd just try once more. They haven't found anyone to look after him, and they fly out on Sunday.'

Hearing the desperate tone in her voice, I realized how selfish I had been and suddenly felt deeply sorry for the poor dog. No animal should ever be put in a cage, let alone for six months and far away from his family.

'All right,' I said. 'I suppose the least I could do is meet him, but I can't promise you anything.'

Nicole sounded ecstatic. I asked her where Chloe and Paul lived, thinking I would ride over when my bike was ready. What she said next made the hairs on my neck stand up and I nearly dropped my phone. I was miles out of town, far from where I live. And I only went there once a year to have my motorbike serviced. But that day, at that precise moment when she rang, I was standing about two minutes' walk from Chloe and Paul's house!

I often wonder what it must feel like to be 90 and to look back on my life from the comfort of my favourite rocking chair. What would I regret the most? What would I be most proud of? What would my happiest memory be? The first two I can't answer yet. The third is easy.

Chloe and Paul answered the door together and almost fell into my arms with excitement. I tried to calm them down and explained I was only there to meet Tyson and I hadn't agreed to look after him. But my words trailed off into stunned silence when I saw behind them, bounding toward me like a giant woolly bear, the happiest, most strikingly beautiful dog I have ever seen. Tyson, all big boofy paws and wagging tail, bowled straight past Chloe and Paul and leapt into my arms like a long-lost lover, kissing me and licking me and sending me tumbling backwards against the door.

To this day I don't know if he knew I was his saviour from the dreaded cage, or if he recognized me immediately as his soulmate. All I know is that it was love at first sight – for both of us! For me, as we hugged each other, it felt like coming home – or, to be more accurate, like finding my home for the first time after 42 years of searching for it. In that instant something shifted inside me. I didn't know what it was at the time, but, looking back, I know now it was the moment my healing began.

When I think back about the way we met – and the fact that, today, Nicole says she still doesn't know why she pushed and pushed so hard for it to happen – it is clear to me that Tyson and I were destined to be together.

Chloe and Paul dropped him off at our house on Saturday, along with their cat, Ginola, a huge, Garfield-like ginger tom whom Nicole had forgotten to mention and who also needed to be cared for and put on a plane with Tyson in six months' time. It was immediately apparent that Tyson and Ginola weren't like other dogs and cats. They had grown up together and were more than just best friends – they were like brothers.

They cuddled together, kissed each other often and even slept on the same bed, with Ginola curled up against Tyson's stomach. Throughout the years they lived with Dana and me, and then, after we broke up, with me on my own, Tyson would always tend to Ginola's wounds after he got into a scrap with one of the neighbourhood cats, which he did quite often. As soon as Ginola came home, Tyson would hold him down gently with one paw while he licked his cuts clean. And if ever Ginola was out on the tiles and Tyson heard the sound of a catfight, he would leap up – even from a deep sleep by the fire – and run out into the garden, where he would bark loudly and watch the top of the fence at the end of the garden until Ginola eventually returned home.

Sometimes Tyson would wait for an hour or more, never relaxing until he saw Ginola scramble back over the fence and plop noisily to the ground. The unwavering loyalty and kindness Tyson showed Ginola taught me the true meaning of friendship in a way no book, no seminar and no human being had ever done, or ever could. I know that if I can show my friends – and my supposed enemies – even a quarter of the loyalty and love Tyson showed his 'little brother', I shall live a very rich and happy life indeed.

From the day Tyson gallumped his way into our lives with his eternally wagging tail, massive bear hugs and unquenchable enthusiasm, Dana and I knew it was going to break our hearts to have to say goodbye to him in just six short months. In fact, after only one week it was impossible to imagine life without him. Everywhere I went, Tyson would walk calmly by my side with no need for a lead or a collar. He would stop at roads, obey all commands and wait patiently outside shops until I came out again. Passersby would invariably marvel at how handsome he was and how immaculately well-behaved and friendly he was as well. No matter whom he met, Tyson would always go straight up to them and lean on them, giving his love without caution or condition.

'Where can I get a dog like that?' they would ask. But I had to explain that, unbelievably, he had been abandoned as a puppy by his first owner and had been rescued from a pound (by Chloe), which meant he had been neutered. Sadly, I would tell them, there could never be a 'Son of Tyson'!

From day one, Tyson and I were inseparable. At picnics and barbecues, friends and strangers alike commented on how perfectly matched he and I were and how he was so obviously 'my' dog. Then, after I told them he wasn't my dog and I was only minding him for a short while, they would say, 'Well, he should be. You're perfect together.' My thoughts exactly!

Dana got the same treatment. Tyson absolutely adored her, and wherever they went people would comment on the strength of their bond. But as the months flew by and the dreaded day grew closer and closer, Dana and I grew more despondent. We thought seriously about moving house and just disappearing with Tyson and Ginola where no one could find us. But we also knew how much Chloe loved both of them and that it would be grossly unfair. No, there really was no way we could prevent the inevitable from happening. Then one day, a light bulb went off in my head. I knew the purpose of life is to learn and grow, so I looked at our predicament from that perspective – and in a flash I realized that the lesson we were supposed to be learning from Tyson and Ginola was to live in the moment. Like life, nothing lasts forever. We only have so many days, so rather than spend our lives worrying about dying, we are supposed to enjoy every moment we can while we are here. Our six months with Tyson were a microcosm of that. Rather than mope around knowing that one day it would be over, we decided to relish every moment we had with him while we could.

And as soon as we got that lesson, we were rewarded with a miracle.

Just two weeks before D-Day, Dana and I were sitting at home one evening watching television. Ginola was asleep in her lap and Tyson was asleep at my feet when the phone rang. I answered it, and Dana knew immediately who it was by my expression.

We hadn't spoken to Chloe for several months, and all I could think was that she was calling to make sure the boys were all set for their big journey. But this is what she said, 'Simon. I'm so sorry to put this on you, but Paul and I have split up and we are both moving out of our house. I know this is a lot to ask, but would you by any chance be able to keep Tyson and Ginola as we can't look after them here?'

It took every ounce of restraint I possessed to commiserate with Chloe and get off the phone as quickly as I could before the volcano of joy erupted inside me and I danced around the room shouting and laughing and crying all at once. Dana and I whooped and hugged each other, tears rolling down our faces. We hugged Tyson and Ginola so tightly we must have squeezed them half to death! In all my 51 years, I never received a better phone call. And I know I never will. Most important of all, I have never forgotten the lesson we both learned about living in the moment – and the fact that when we learn such an important lesson, our angels always reward us immediately with a gift of pure joy.

One morning, about a year later, just after Christmas, I was up early and sitting on the patio making notes for a book I was writing at the time about the dynamics of human relationships and why they so often break down. The chapter on which I was working dealt with the agony and confusion that many people feel when they start to doubt whether their partner truly loves them because they just don't feel loved by them. Tyson, as ever, was at my feet, looking up at me with his big, wise brown eyes, waiting patiently for me to take him for a walk. As I smiled at him, a question popped into my head. It almost felt as though he put it there via telepathy, or something. 'Why do I love you so much?' I said out loud, bending down to kiss him on his nose. 'I mean, you are the gentlest, kindest and most loving dog in the world. But you never tell me you love me, and you never buy me things or take me places to show me you love me!'

And then it hit me.

I loved Tyson so much because he LET me love him!

It was that simple. I kissed his nose again in delight and started to write as fast as I could as the words literally poured out of me onto the page. So many people feel unloved by their partners because their partners disappear into themselves whenever a challenge arises. That's how some people deal with things, but it leaves the other person feeling abandoned and unloved. We all crave openness. We want our partners to be fully present, to share their feelings with us and to open up the deepest, darkest recesses of their hearts. But so many people are uncomfortable with that. It makes them feel vulnerable.

And besides, they mistakenly think that what we really want is for them to be strong, and that involves shutting down their emotions – closing up their hearts, if you will – so that they can 'get the job done'. Sure, we love a strong partner who makes us feel safe and protected, but not if it means they shut themselves off from their emotions, thus denying us the opportunity to love them at the deepest level. You see, the bottom line is: it feels better to love someone than to be loved by someone. We long to be able to love fully, and if our partner doesn't let us – by not opening up – we will take this as evidence they don't truly love us.

The terrible irony is that throughout all this, the other person believes they are being a good partner. They love us. Take care of us. Work hard to provide us with all we want. Even tell us they love us over and over again. And they simply cannot understand why we say we don't feel loved! This fundamental misunderstanding can quickly turn to resentment, which turns to anger and fighting, and worse. And, often as not, we split up, thinking the other person didn't truly love us, while they're left thinking we must be mad because all they did was love us. If only they had simply opened up their heart and let us love them!

By doing this, of course, they are not actually 'doing' anything at all, which is why it almost never occurs to them. It is entirely passive and yet can make us feel as though we are actively being loved.

A few days later, at a New Year's Eve party, I shared my insight with a man I met who had confided in me that he was having some difficulties with his relationship. As soon as I had finished, his eyes lit up. He handed me his drink, thanked me profusely and rushed off to find his wife. I watched him run up to a beautiful woman sitting all by herself and give her a long, tender hug, and I knew instantly that Tyson had saved their marriage.

Sadly, my relationship with Dana couldn't be saved. We went our different ways, but our love for Tyson has kept us together and today, seven years later, we are closer than ever. I am also proud to count Dana's boyfriend, David, as one of my dearest friends. Everyone I have met in the past seven years – and I mean everyone – who learns that Dana and I lived together for four years is flabbergasted at how we have managed not only to stay close friends, but to grow our love and friendship to an even deeper level. They all ask me how on Earth we did it. And I always give them the same one-word answer: Tyson. You see, after we broke up, whatever feelings we may have had about each other were always of secondary importance to the need to care for Tyson. Ginola, being a cat, was much more adaptable. But Tyson was a very sensitive soul and he absolutely loved Dana as much as he loved me, so it was important that he spend a lot of time with both of us. The conversation of who should have Tyson never once came up. Dana and I never spoke about it even for a second because we both knew that he was neither 'her dog' nor 'my dog' – he was an angel who had come into both our lives, and wherever he was needed was where he would be.

I know how much Tyson helped Dana immediately after we broke up and then when she moved north to live with David, Tyson came to live with me. And that's how he was able to heal both our hearts.

Whenever I went away, Tyson stayed with Dana and David. And as often as I could, I would drive him to their house three hours north of Sydney on a weekend so he could spend a whole week with them, and they would drive him back the following weekend.

To give you an idea of how much he loved Dana, four years after we broke up Tyson and I were walking down the main street of the suburb where I lived and we both heard the distinctive 'beep beep' sound of someone disarming their car alarm by remote control. It was exactly the same alarm that Dana had had on her old car, which she had sold several years earlier. Despite it being years since he had heard that sound, Tyson's ears pricked up immediately and his eyes opened wide with an ecstatic expression of 'Mum!' In a flash he was off, running up and down the street as fast as his legs could carry him, searching for her.

I called after him that it wasn't his mum, but he ignored me. He raced up and down the rows of cars for a good 20 minutes before I could get him to agree, reluctantly, that it wasn't Mum's car, and he eventually followed me home with a pitifully forlorn look on his face, the kind of 'woe is me' expression only genuinely sad dogs are capable of, and no human can ever hope to emulate!

Tyson lived with me for seven years before he died, and in all that time he always welcomed everyone who came to the house with the same joyful greeting. But there was a very special welcome he reserved just for Dana. He literally turned cartwheels and jumped for joy every single time he heard the distinctive sound of her voice calling his name from the car as she pulled into the driveway. I'm told he did the same thing when I went to pick him up from her house. So you see, Dana and I could do nothing but love each other, when the object of our adoration loved both of us so much. Our deep and enduring friendship is yet another of Tyson's legacies and a lesson to us – and all of you – that love never has to die. The years I lived with Tyson have been the happiest of my life by far. And in all that time he taught me so many valuable lessons about patience, loyalty and unconditional love, just by being himself.

But the most powerful and life-changing lesson of all he decided to save for last.

I knew Tyson was getting old and that my nightmare was not far from becoming a reality. He was 13, which for his two breeds and his size was well above the average life expectancy. His arthritis meant he had trouble getting up from his bed, and he walked very slowly. And he had a brain tumour that caused him to have terrifying seizures like epileptic fits every few weeks. But he never complained once, and he never showed even a hint of grumpiness right up to the end – another lesson that we humans would do well to learn! The most difficult challenge of having a pet is the knowledge that one day you will have to say goodbye to them. We love them like our children, and yet when we have a child we assume that the natural order of things is for us to die before they do. We love them like our husband or wife, and yet when we fall in love we never think about who is going to go first. Not so with a pet. Right from the start we know that, barring some tragedy, we will have to bury them one day. And the pain of that is almost too much to bear. I was never able to even contemplate life without Tyson. He was my partner, my son and my whole world. And I knew that when the day came, I would fall apart. But Tyson had other ideas.

One Monday morning, about two months after his 13th birthday, I took him in to be washed by the groomer who worked at the vet surgery just up the road where Tyson always went when he was sick. The vets and nurses who work there had become Tyson's second family. They adored him like he was their own, and they always gave him special treatment. In Tyson's later years I decided to have him washed at the vet surgery rather than at a grooming salon, just in case anything happened – in which case he would be in the right place to get immediate expert care. That turned out to be one of the best decisions I have ever made.

A few hours after I dropped him off, I got a call from the vet saying that Tyson was having trouble breathing. I rushed over at once and found him in the surgery being examined by two of the emergency doctors. Tyson was by now completely unable to breathe and was starting to turn blue, so they knocked him out with a powerful anaesthetic and placed an oxygen tube into his mouth and down his windpipe. We then rushed him across town to the emergency 24-hour veterinary hospital where he could receive round-the-clock care. The first thing the doctors did was shave him from head to claw – including his tail, his ears, face and paws – in case he had been bitten by a paralysis tic, an all-too-common occurrence in Australia. There was no tic. Instead, a CT scan later revealed that the tumour in his brain had ruptured and this was what had caused him to be partially paralyzed.

For three days the doctors fought to save him. A nurse told me later that in her ten years at the hospital she had never seen them try so hard or care so much for a patient. It didn't surprise me – Tyson had that effect on everyone he met! But by Thursday, although he had recovered the ability to breathe and eat, most of his body was still paralyzed and I was told he would never sit or walk again.

They also said that if the tumour ruptured again, it would likely be fatal. I asked the doctors to give me some time alone with him and lay down on the floor next to Tyson for what seemed like hours, crying and holding him until I plucked up the courage to ask him if he wanted to stay or go.

He was drugged, shaved, paralyzed, terrified and exhausted, and yet that eternally loving and devoted look was still there on his handsome face as he gazed deep into my tear-filled eyes. It was not a look of pain, or self-pity – but of pure love for me. I will never forget it. And it told me all I needed to know. Dana and David were on holiday in Indonesia and they jumped on the first plane back to Sydney, which was due to land early on Saturday.

That morning I drove Tyson home very slowly from the hospital on his final journey. I carried him into the house and laid him down on his bed, which I had moved into the living room and surrounded with all his favourite toys and teddies. He looked so frail without any fur, and although he could move his head a little, his body was broken and motionless. I did my best to be cheerful for him, singing to him and cuddling him until Dana and David's taxi arrived from the airport. For the next four hours, the three of us stroked and kissed Tyson and thanked him over and over again for all the joy and love and wisdom he had given

117

us. He was completely calm, despite not being able to move, and was clearly happy to be home again and to be surrounded by his family. Ginola came in and gave him a kiss, and with a determined effort Tyson lifted up his head and gave his little brother one last lingering lick.

There is no doubt in my mind that Tyson knew exactly what was happening. In the hospital the night before, I had spent hours lying with him, explaining that in the morning he was going to come home, and then he was going to go home. I knew he understood.

Nicole arrived and joined in the hugs. She was the reason we had been blessed to have Tyson in our lives in the first place. She had brought us all together; she was part of his family, and we wanted her to be there. She brought out some delicious chicken she had cooked specially for him, and together we gave Tyson his last meal, which he wolfed down with a wonderful final burst of puppy energy. Then it was time.

The vet arrived with a nurse. As she injected the fatal overdose, all four of us held Tyson and smiled and kissed him and told him how much we loved him. I looked into his eyes and said over and over again, 'Thank you, thank you, thank you! Thank you for choosing to share your life with me. Thank you for all your love. Thank you, darling. Thank you!'

Tyson didn't even notice the deadly liquid being pushed into him through the catheter in his leg. And his eyes never flinched or broke contact with mine even for a second as it raced through his veins toward his heart. Then, at the exact moment that it hit and he slipped away, two things happened that changed the lives of everyone in the room forever. The front door suddenly swung open with a loud bang, and a split second later, despite his tail being paralyzed from the stroke he had suffered five days earlier, Tyson wagged it strongly four or five times, and then was gone. It was not physically possible, but it happened.

In an instant, our tears of sadness turned to tears of joy because we knew he was safe. He must have seen an angel come for him and had somehow managed to wag his tail just as he passed over into spirit form. Earlier in the day I had asked my father, who had died many years before, to come and get Tyson and make sure he was all right. So whether it was him, or an angel, who came in through the front door, I don't know, and it doesn't matter. All that matters is that we quite literally saw Tyson going up into Heaven, and what was left behind was nothing more than an empty vessel – a frail, broken old body that had served its purpose well and wasn't needed any more. By showing us this miracle and wagging his tail, Tyson in his own inimitable way had given us one last, life-changing lesson ... that there is a Heaven, and we have nothing to fear from death.

I know that in the years to come, Tyson will continue to teach me and guide me from the spirit world. And I know that when it is my turn, he will be there to welcome me and we will be together again forever. Until that day comes, I will spend my life teaching Tyson's lessons to as many people as I can through my books and my seminars, so that his remarkable love and wisdom can heal others, just as they healed me.

Simon asked me to try and contact Tyson, and this big, brave dog came into my heart immediately. He showed me his name, written in a particular kind of script. When I told Simon, he was delighted, saying that the day after Tyson had passed he'd got a tattoo done on his right wrist, exactly as Tyson had showed me...

CHAPTER 7

Mystical Pets

Animals who can see and communicate with spirits. Telepathic pets

Pets are more closely attuned to their intuition than we humans can even remember being. We should follow their example.

– JENNY SMEDLEY

I'M HERE!

Elise sent me this story.

Shortly after my first marriage, on the day of my 22nd birthday, 19 January 1979, naïve, unworldly and wanting a baby, I went out shopping one Saturday morning with precisely £60 for the week's groceries. Passing the local pet shop on the way to the shops, I caught sight of one lonely, black-and-white puppy in the window. I never did buy any groceries that week, but arrived home, to my husband's dismay, with a six-week-old Border Collie puppy. Dismay due to the fact that we both worked full time, I had no idea how to look after a puppy, let alone a grown dog, and the choice of breed didn't fit in at all with our lifestyle. We called him Patch due to the fact that he had a black patch on the back of his neck, and after a disagreement as to whether we should keep him, it was easier to choose a name that my husband had used to name his own dog years before and fitted our new arrival. Somehow we got by.

I suppose you could say that Patch and I grew up together. I learned responsibility for the first time in my life and how to look after a dependent creature. He had his faults; actually they were my own, due to the fact that I was unable to give him what he needed as a young, growing and extremely intelligent, active dog. Hence, he could be 'naughty' at times. He was, however, my best friend, substitute child and companion for over 16 years. He was the friend who kept me from totally falling apart during an unhappy marriage, loss of a baby, divorce and then loss of employment. To say that he offered the only real stability in my life at that time would be an understatement.

Patch never strayed far from my side. He slept on the bed, lay on the sofa, ate his meals with me and was, I suppose you could say, spoiled. That is, unless you've read any books by Cesar Milan [renowned dog behaviour specialist], in which case you'd probably say I was a pretty lousy dog owner! I admit that I do it very differently these days. My dogs are brought up and looked after as dogs, not humans; they're trained, well-behaved and they don't sleep on the bed and aren't allowed on the sofa! Oh, those were the days, though. We were soulmates of a kind. They say dogs take after their owners, and I firmly believe that to be the case. In those days, I was rather neurotic; hence, I owned a rather neurotic dog! And we adored each other for nine long years, until one day I will never forget in 1987.

I had gone to my mother's house in Esher, Surrey, and taken Patch with me. He pretty well came everywhere with me except for the times I was working or unable to take him, hence, he would often stay at my mother's so he had company until I could collect him. On this particular day I was going to visit a friend in a nearby village and left

Patch in my mother's garden, which backed onto a field where we often walked together. It was some time around mid-afternoon when I left, and I didn't return until about 6 p.m., thinking my mother would have brought Patch back into the house before I arrived to take him home with me to my own house in Byfleet. I let myself in (my mother always insisted her daughters had keys to the family house) and expected Patch to run and greet me as he always did. But he wasn't in the house. 'Mum,' I called, 'I'm back, is Patch still in the garden?'

'I don't know,' she answered. 'I thought he was with you.' And he wasn't in the garden either. In fact, he was nowhere to be found. Patch had simply disappeared. The date was 20 December 1987, five days before Christmas.

It was the worst Christmas I can ever remember. I'd recently lost my job, my lover and now the only real friend, ally, baby, soulmate – my reason for carrying on – had gone. With my family's help, I spent the entire Christmas scouring local fields, villages, woods, river walks – in fact, anywhere we had ever walked together. As I'd been something of a wandering soul (I'd moved several times with Patch), we covered a 25-mile radius of dog walks around most of Surrey. The biggest marketing campaign for one lost dog was immediately under way, with coloured posters and descriptions of him hung in every conceivable location covering Guildford, East Horsley, Molesey, Byfleet and many other villages throughout Surrey; anywhere, in fact, where we'd spent our happiest hours roaming through woods and fields. The internet was still unknown to the vast majority of us in those days, so the only way was to put posters up and get as much as possible into the local newspapers, local radio, vets, wherever it was permissible to advertise a missing pet.

I recall becoming ill just after Christmas and having to take to my bed with a high fever, feeling even worse because I was unable to go out and look for my baby. I wrote long, sad poems mourning the loss of Patch with cries to the universe for angelic or divine assistance. I sent out thought messages to my dog, letting him know if he could hear me that I missed him badly and begging him to be OK until I found him. What astounded me was how much people really cared. The phone calls over that period were profound, from people I didn't know, had never met and may never encounter again. I received offers of assistance from complete strangers who would call and let me know that they were thinking of both Patch and me and would keep a lookout when they were out with their own dogs. Many callers believed that they had seen him and, when I was able to get out again, I visited any area where reports of sightings had been made.

One young couple with enough of their own troubles, a psychologically disturbed young man and his pregnant girlfriend only days away from her due date, insisted that they come out with me and help me search some local fields. I really did feel that there was a little divine intervention in the form of some of the wonderful people who appeared in my life during the worst few weeks I can ever remember. And I was never convinced that I actually deserved anything – after all, what had I ever contributed to the world to help others?

On 28 January 1988 I received a telephone call. Patch had been missing for 39 days. I had received so many calls that at this point I didn't get too excited, but the woman's voice sounded different to all the others. 'I'm calling about the dog,' she said. 'But I can't give you my name because I know who has him and it's too dangerous to tell you who I am.' A little dubious at this point, I asked her how she knew it was my dog. 'Well,' she said, 'he's a black-and-white Border Collie and he's getting a little grey. He was stolen from a field in Esher before Christmas and I know who stole him.' Now I really was listening. 'The man who took him is a drug dealer and lives in Kingston. Your dog's still there. I've heard him bragging about the dog he stole in Esher and he's brought him to the pub.' She was frightened to tell me who she was even though a reward was offered for any information, and I got the feeling she really could do with that reward, although it was more important to her that I found my dog. It was as though she knew what I was going through. Perhaps she'd been through something similar and could empathize. People who are able to feel acutely for others, and I felt she had probably been through her own traumatic experience of loss. Whoever she was, as far as I was concerned this woman was a true angel or had certainly been sent by an angel.

Patch had been reported missing at all the local police stations, but as this was the Kingston-upon-Thames area, after a brief conversation with Esher police they informed me that I would have to speak to Kingston police. Sod that, I thought, and with my lodger, a charming young man (I shall call him Tim) who had been totally supportive throughout the few weeks of trauma, I drove to Kingston Police Station. I was in quite a state by this point, desperately needing to find out if Patch was where this woman had said he was and quite prepared to go with my lodger alone to the address she had given me. The police, however, had other ideas. 'Now, now, you can't go off to this estate on your own, and how do you know that this is your dog anyway?' they said and took us into an interview room where I would need to give more details. 'Well,' said I, 'let me give you an accurate description, then you can check for yourselves,' getting more and more agitated. 'No. 1 – he has a white muzzle with a white stripe down the middle of his black head; he has a white chest and stomach. No. 2 – he has three black legs with white socks; the front left leg is white with black spots. No. 3 – he has a white tip on the end of a black bushy tail; he has a black diamond-shaped patch on his neck. And No. 4 … he has no balls!'

'Whoa … calm down, love. We just have to make sure before we go barging into someone's flat that we have something concrete to go in with … OK, OK … let's get a squad car.'

Three policemen, one squad car, a very agitated, verging-on-hysterical woman and her lodger drove through Kingston at about 8 p.m. that evening. That nearly hysterical woman sat in the squad car with Tim and one policeman while the other two policemen went into a flat in a block nearby. It seemed like an eternity and I am unsure exactly how long they were gone but at some point I saw them coming back to the car … smiling. 'Now love, we need you to stay calm … I think we've found your dog.' And as calmly as I could, leaving Tim in the car with the driver, I went with the two policemen into the block of flats and up to a front door on the second floor. 'We need to warn you,' one said. 'This man is on drugs and he's not quite there. His girlfriend is also in the flat and fairly drugged as well, so we'll just go in so that you can identify the dog.'

Patch barely recognized me and looked as if he, too, had been given drugs or was so traumatized by whatever he had experienced that he could only just stand up and wobble over to me with a slightly glazed look and a half-hearted lift of his tail. I burst into tears at that point and put my arms around my beloved pet. The police asked if I wished to press charges but, looking at the state of the two people in the flat, I said that they had probably suffered enough. The man was in tears, begging my forgiveness and claiming that he hadn't had any idea what he had really done, and the woman was so out of it that I don't believe she even knew what was going on. I just wanted to get home with Patch, get him checked by the vet as soon as possible and have him back by my side. We had to return to the police station to make a further statement and then took Patch home where he remained, eyes glazed and detached, for a couple of days. The vet found nothing seriously wrong with him, although Tim was convinced that he had been abused, due to a strange reaction when the dog saw him taking his belt off to change.

However, Patch bounced back to his old self fairly quickly and we resumed some semblance of normal life once more. It transpired that the man had been fishing by the river in the field behind my mother's house and had driven his car into the field. Patch had jumped the wall at the back of my mother's garden and, seeing an open car door (he was crazy about cars and would frequently jump into any car with an open door!), he had simply jumped in and the man had driven off with him, removing his name disc and collar first. So he had, in fact, known exactly what he was doing!

Patch remained a major part of my life as my best friend and soulmate for almost another seven years until he finally passed on at the grand old age of 16 in July 1995. If it hadn't been for the help of all those wonderful people, the local newspapers and especially the woman who had read an article, I believe in the *Esher News and Mail*, written by Animal Lifeline (Surrey) – a registered charity for animal rescue, who I have no doubt were sent by the angels, the universe or whatever – I would not have found Patch. It is in writing this story that I wish to express my profound and sincere thanks to all for their help and love, albeit somewhat belatedly! The faith I kept in the possibility of divine intervention throughout that time was rewarded in full in the form of humanity at its most loving and the return to me of my beloved dog, Patch.

The reason I've included this story here is that I believe Patch did get some sort of message from his owner Elise, and that perhaps he somehow managed to get through to the woman who informed on the 'dognapper'. When she saw the dog in the pub, I believe she was overwhelmed with a sense that she had to get this dog back to where he belonged, and this is why she didn't feel inclined to accept any reward either.

A SILENT GOODBYE

Amanda's story is about telepathic communication with a dearly loved pet.

I've seen nearly all my cats – Tigger the ginger-and-white moggy, Whiska my black little huntress, and Spooky my grey girl – after they've died. They were cats we had when I was growing up, and I'd see glimpses of them around our old house every now and then. I think it was after Whiska died – she was run over – that I was lying in bed one night and I felt her jump up onto the bed and curl up on my chest. We didn't have any cats at that time so there was no logical explanation for that.

I also had a black kitten, Raphael, when I was about 12, who 'told' me telepathically that he was very sick and was going to die soon. I told my parents but they didn't believe me, and we went on holiday for a week (I had to be dragged away, crying) while my grandparents came to cat-sit. When I came back, he'd died – I think it was leukaemia, but I know the vet was sufficiently worried it might be too dangerous a virus to perform an autopsy. I saw Raphael about for a bit after he passed, too.

EXACTLY WHERE I'M MEANT TO BE

Tracey takes care of other people's dogs in her home, but some mean more to her than others.

It was definitely love at first sight. Not the holiday romance kind, which is great while it lasts but is soon forgotten. This was the heart-stopping, life-changing, forever kind. When Misty first walked into our kitchen on Thursday 26 March 2009, I instantly knew she was a very special little dog indeed: a beautiful six-year-old Cocker Spaniel with a gleaming black velvety coat, huge shiny brown eyes and the most amazing character.

The other dogs didn't make the usual move forward to investigate and sniff her bottom; instead they quietly watched her enter the room and kept a respectful distance while she calmly looked around and then settled regally into her bed. They too knew we had a very special guest. It was like the Queen had popped in for a visit. Queen Misty had entered the building.

That first time she stayed for just three nights, which were over far too quickly. I admit it: I fall in love with every dog who stays for home-boarding. I love them, and then I have to hand them back. I had been getting better at the handing-back bit, and I usually recovered quite quickly, but thoughts of little Misty were never far from my mind. I was over the moon when her owner booked her in again for a two-week stay in April.

Those two weeks were warm and sunny and we had some fabulous walks with Misty, our own dog, Layla, and all the other visiting dogs. In the evenings I'd sit on the living room floor for the customary group cuddle with them all, and my husband would raise an eyebrow as Misty always had prime position on my lap, one paw either side of my neck while I showered her shiny black nose with kisses. When the dreaded day came, I sat on a bench in the garden on a lovely sunny afternoon, waiting for her owner to arrive. Misty-Moo was on my lap, snuggled into my neck and snoring gently. Her black coat was warm from the sun. All too soon the time came, and she jumped from my lap eager to be reunited with her owner. I watched the reunion with mixed emotions: happy that she was happy, sad to see her go.

We see some doggies just once a year, but we only had to wait until July to see Misty again. I counted the days until she arrived, and my heart leapt when I saw her trotting down the driveway. Even Layla, the Black Beast of Dartmoor, couldn't contain her pleasure at the sight of her pal and proceeded to wash Misty's face while Misty sat quietly, taking all the adoration in her stride.

As usual she settled in beautifully, got on with all the other doggies who came and went, and it was clear there was a strong bond growing between her and Layla. On walks, Layla would charge into the woods after squirrels with Misty hot on her heels. Misty's little legs would be going ten to the dozen to keep up with her longer-legged friend, and they would re-emerge minutes later panting and excited from the chase.

I made sure I was out when Misty-Moo was collected. I cried as we said our goodbyes that morning, certain it would be a long time before we met again. I cuddled her close to me and told her how much I loved her as she licked the tears from my cheeks. My husband rang me to tell me she'd been collected. My heart broke a little as I wondered if I would ever see her again. Then I couldn't believe what I was hearing as he told me, 'Misty may have to be re-homed. Her owner asked if we knew of anyone who might want to give her a good home...'

Misty arrived three weeks later, at 2 p.m. on Sunday 3 August. Her lovely owner was heartbroken to hand her over, and it was incredibly emotional. Now it's like she's always been ours and I can't imagine life without her. Dreams do come true...

I really think that when Misty realized the extent of the love Tracey had to offer her, and once she'd understood the concept of what was going on, she influenced her owner to let her make Tracey's dream come true.

TOBIE THE LIFE-SAVER

Gemma has many reasons to thank her dog, Tobie.

I think that my dog Tobie sees spirits because on some night-times his ears and nose suddenly start to twitch and he goes onto the landing and sits barking and growling at thin air. I check outside and downstairs, but there's nothing there. He then seems to be stalking something, but I can see nothing. He also saved us once. One day we left the gas on in the shop above which we live, and Tobie wouldn't stop barking that night. When we woke up we found him scratching at the door to get down into the shop. We opened the door, let him into the shop downstairs and he ran straight to the cooker where the gas was on. He jumped and scratched at the cooker, and I tried to go and switch it off, but Tobie wouldn't let me go near it. He was rounding me up like a sheep and herding me away from the danger. Eventually I persuaded him to let me reach the cooker and turn off the gas, and then he calmed down. If Tobie hadn't warned me, I could have died in my sleep from carbon monoxide poisoning, or I might have lit a cigarette and blown the place up. Tobie will also come and tell me if the bath-water is about to overflow. He really is my little star.

CHAPTER 8

Wild Animals

Is the fox a cold-blooded killer? Does the lion feel sorry for its prey? Are animals innocent?

A long time ago … man knew that Nature was not 'wild' and hostile but was a benevolent friend. Then, by a twist of organized religious dogma, many began to think humans are the greatest and most important part of creation and they saw Nature as 'fallen' and sinful. Man has attempted to divorce himself from Nature to the detriment of all creation…

Animals know the time and place to migrate, but man cannot find his way without a compass or the stars. Animals live well without the need of

tools or weapons. Man cannot. Animals are happy
and contented in their environment. Man is not.
Animals live among their families all their lives.
Man does not. Animals have found the right way to
live with their limitations and skills without rancor
or strife. Man has not.

– GRANDFATHER LEE STANDING BEAR MOORE
(THROUGH HIS FRIEND TAKATOKA)

I asked a question above – is the fox a cold-blooded killer?
Well, in a way yes, it is, because unlike humans, who know
exactly what they're doing when they harm an animal or
another person, and often commit crime out of anger, a
fox or any other predator is unable to put itself in its prey's
shoes and doesn't act out of emotion, so in a way they are
'cold-blooded' about killing. They merely follow their survival instinct. What they do is not premeditated, and they
have no conception that their actions may cause pain and
suffering to the other creature. The question should perhaps be, 'Are foxes cold-blooded *murderers*?' The answer in
this case is no. When a fox is presented with a cage full of
chickens, it doesn't act out of bloodlust. A better analogy
would be that of a child let loose in a sweet shop and told
to help himself. We can't blame him if he reacts to that

stimulus. It's we humans who hunt and kill foxes, hares and deer for our own enjoyment. It's we who kill other humans in the grip of anger or hatred. Man is the only animal capable of murder.

I've often said that animals are in many ways more spiritual than we are. I say this taking into account many factors:

- Intent – animals don't act with malice the way humans do. In this way they are innocent of what might be perceived as 'barbaric' acts of cruelty or the 'crimes' of assault or killing. When they kill they do it for survival and no emotion plays a part in their actions. Even animals who fight each other, such as stags, don't do so because they're angry or feeling violent or because they hate the other stag. They do it out of instinct, for the survival of their species, to make sure only the fittest specimens mate and procreate.

- Animals don't show prejudice the way humans do. An animal won't act differently to another animal because its coat is a different colour. They won't attack it because the other animal has a bent ear or is scarred, or tease and torment it because it is deemed to be ugly or fat or stupid.

- People have a problem being open enough or relaxed enough to receive angelic or spiritual communication. Animals have no problem at all with falling into meditation or sleep, so long as their basic physical needs are met, whereas humans, because we don't live in the moment, are always too concerned with the past and the future to be able to switch off.

- Animals retain their connection to Nature and have heightened their intuition and instincts, whereas the human race in general has stifled theirs.

In the 2004 tsunami, tragically, 220,000 people were killed. This was mostly because they had no warning whatsoever. There were even people on the beach looking at the sea as it was gathering itself to sweep them away. Almost no animals were killed, and only two wild animal fatalities were reported. Two trained elephants even broke free of their restraints and escaped to higher ground, surprising their keepers who had no idea why the animals were behaving strangely. When you add to this the fact that this happened an hour *before* the tsunami struck, it destroys the argument that the animals could somehow hear the approaching wave. Some people were saved because they ran after their dogs, who were fleeing the area. The flood waters travelled two miles inland, destroying a wildlife park, and yet no corpses of animals were ever found, and it appears they all escaped the waters. This tells us that animals are more connected to Nature than we are, because they haven't abandoned their natural abilities the way we have, in favour of relying on technology.

Animals don't hold grudges and will instantly forgive those they love. They don't harbour the guilt to which we cling and which can destroy our spirituality from the inside out. When they love, they truly love unconditionally, with no barriers of gender, sexual orientation, age, size, shape or colour.

I recently watched on TV the story of a baby hippopotamus (a species which is recognized as the world's most dangerous animal) which was adopted after being orphaned and which has grown up to live in and around the house of her adoptive parents. She gets along fine with the household dogs and even caresses and washes their puppies, which she could easily crush and swallow in an instant. She swims with her human 'parents' and sleeps on a blanket at night to be close to them. The love this animal has for her carers is indisputable.

So, I ask you, which species can be judged to have the better energy, and to be closer to God, us or the animals?

CHAPTER 9

Abuse of Animals

Is it wrong to perceive animals as here merely for human consumption and sport? Does intensively farming animals harm the soul of the person who does it?

A long time ago, humans were created to be caretakers of the garden – Mother Earth. They held all things of creation sacred. The people respected Nature and understood they were only a small part of the whole circle of life. Humans knew each part of creation played a significant role in the contentment and survival of the other. They accepted the divine idea that all things were equal and no animal, including man, held dominion over other parts of creation.

American Indians, also known as the People of the Land, traditionally and historically hold a special knowledge of the land and its inhabitants. Intimate knowledge of the world surrounding the American Indian was possible because of a belief system that considered all things of creation equal and necessary, worthy of respect and honour.

– **GRANDFATHER LEE STANDING BEAR MOORE**
(THROUGH HIS FRIEND TAKATOKA)

What was it that triggered such arrogance in humans that we should start to believe that we could treat animals in any way we saw fit, regardless of their senses or feelings, and that our actions wouldn't have a knock-on effect on us and our souls?

Grandfather Lee Standing Bear Moore goes on to say:

American Indians view all things in creation as having spiritual energy. All things are connected and worthy of our respect and reverence. Our way is to seek balance and harmony within the complex tapestry of life called the Great Circle of Life. As we move within the circle, we emphasize these truths:

Everything on Earth is alive.

Everything on Earth has purpose.
Everything on Earth is connected.
Everything on Earth is to be embraced.
A principal tenet of our belief is that all things are connected and we are related to all things in the circle.

This is something that the human race in general has forgotten. Native Americans do still kill animals for food, but they do it with respect and with gratitude for the animals' sacrifice. I recently had to turn off a TV show because it featured celebrities playing 'games' that involved the spurious use of dead animals' heads and eyes in the name of entertainment. By performing this kind of disrespectful crudity I'm afraid mankind is bringing itself closer and closer to the edge of self-destruction. I feel huge compassion for anyone who works in intensive farming, or badly run and cruel abattoirs or laboratories, because I believe they're severely damaging their own souls' energy and progress by doing that kind of work. I feel especially sorry for people who've been forced into that kind of work against their principles, in desperation, in order to support their families.

The UK Government has recently called for CCTV cameras to be installed in all abattoirs to ensure that animals are treated kindly, and I think that's a very good idea both for the animals and the people who work there. One of the reasons animals have been put together with humans on this world is for the humans to help the animals' souls get ready for their ultimate challenge: being encased in a human body and mind and retaining their spiritual integrity. In order for this to happen, an animal's soul must be encouraged to be free of fear. We've been entrusted with this task by the universe. To abuse that trust and do the complete opposite of what we're supposed to do, by creating pain, terror and dread in the animals – specifically the pain we humans ourselves inflict – invites a karmic response that we might well come to regret.

I have had personal experience of the way the energy from an abattoir can also spread throughout the local area. When we first moved to Somerset, the village we were in seemed nice and the people friendly, so we couldn't understand it when it seemed to us that the whole place started to get dark in terms of energy. With the advent of the foot and mouth outbreak things got worse very quickly, with the wholesale slaughter of all the hundreds of sheep in and around the village. Eventually we had to move, for our peace of mind, and it was only then that we learned there was an abattoir a little way out of the village, tucked away down a hidden side road. That explained everything. So, if you're scouting out a new area to live in, don't make our mistake: check the surroundings and the businesses out thoroughly.

For a long time animals were considered to be devoid of feelings and emotions, and in particular any suggestion that one animal could grieve for the loss of another would be laughed at. Earlier in this book I've already recounted the story of the cat who tried to administer a kind of CPR to bring his friend back to life, but for those more scientifically minded there are further examples to be found.

A scientific research paper has recently been published chronicling three captive chimpanzees; they are called Blossom, Rosie and Chippy. They had a forth companion called Pansy, but during the time of the observations, Pansy became very ill and subsequently died. The chimps were allowed to stay with Pansy as she died, and their behaviour immediately after her death ranged from attempts to make her arms and legs move, and close inspections of her mouth, to an actual 'attack' by the male, Chippy, in what observers say closely resembled an attempt at revival, perhaps a kind of CPR. Rosie was Pansy's daughter and she sat by her mother's body all night, while Blossom tried to console Chippy, grooming and cuddling him for hours. Then they watched as Pansy's body was removed from the sleeping platform and the area was cleaned and disinfected. For the next five nights, none of the chimps would enter the sleeping area, and all of them slept outside in the day area. This had never happened previously to Pansy's death. To read the full report, please see the website listed in the Resources chapter.

This is only one of many examples of apes who have displayed classic grief symptoms. If you'd like more, just put in an internet search for 'grieving in chimps' and you'll find not only written accounts but also photographs and video footage of the behaviour.

Like most people who have animals in their lives, I have had to have some put to sleep humanely. The responses of my dogs have been very interesting. On occasion in the early days, when I didn't know better and a pet would be euthanized out of sight of the other pets and its body removed, the remaining dogs would take weeks to get over the loss, constantly looking for their missing friend and lying on the passed-away dog's bed or toys as if in an attempt to get close to their lost companion. Nowadays, if this has to happen, I allow the other dogs to be close to their dying friend. I've found this has made their responses quite different. They have watched quietly, with apparent sorrow, and then, having sniffed the dead body carefully, they will walk away and show no further signs of really missing the dead dog.

It seems to me that this reveals two things: one, that the dogs are able to understand and even perhaps see their friend's spirit leave the body, and so the flesh loses interest for them once that has gone, and two, that they understand that their companion is not lost, but has moved on to a place where they will one day go, too.

I'm very pleased that as I write this, I'm looking at a newspaper cutting that says Spain has begun the process of banning bullfighting. The region of Catalonia has started the ball rolling and I hope the rest of the country follows suit. Just like the ban on hunting with dogs here in the UK has its supporters and opposition, so does Spain's new stance on bullfighting. In my opinion both of these things and some others need to be consigned to the history books to go the way of dogfighting and bear-baiting, both for the good of the animals and the good of the human souls that partake in it. Animals are not here to be made sport of, or hunted to exhaustion, or killed wholesale in appalling conditions for food.

The human race has already come close to all-out war with Nature, a war we will surely lose, and we need to take several steps backwards, the first of which is to start treating the animals who share this planet with us with the same respect we would like ourselves.

CHAPTER 10

Time Travel with Your Pet

How to rewrite your pets' scripts to heal their illnesses and apparent behaviour problems that have been generated by past-life energy and current life trauma

When one becomes linked to a pet's subconscious, it's better than a Vulcan mind meld — and who knows what miracles may spontaneously occur?

– JENNY SMEDLEY

As much as life with a pet can be filled with inspiration and love, sometimes, even with the best intentions, things seem to go disastrously wrong. Pets develop illnesses involving expensive and time-consuming visits to the vet's, and also behavioural issues. Why is this?

Many animal communicators, of which I am one, believe that these issues can often be found to have originated in previous lifetimes. I've already mentioned that some pets have been with us before, and this has been borne out by a great deal of anecdotal evidence. Many of us also believe that your pet, if he is spiritually attached to you, can manifest physical symptoms in order to try and bring your attention to a problem whose root lies in your spiritual depths. Indeed, I'd even say that an animal can specifically decide to reincarnate to be with you in order to bring such a thing to your attention. Once you've accepted this premise then you can proceed to 'rewrite the script' with your pet.

So how does this work, and how can you use it to solve problems? The first thing you can do is to try and equate the issues your pet is having with any obvious or underlying issues you may have yourself. For instance, if your pet has a health issue, look into what impact and correlation there might be between you and the site of the problem.

Here are a few examples:

- **Abdominal and digestive problems** in your pet can mean that you are repressing your emotions. Past-life issues that are blocking you are something from which you have closed yourself off. You need to investigate these issues and meet them head-on in order to move on.

- **Teeth problems**, when recurrent in your pet, can be a sign that you need to put the past firmly behind you, by healing it and making a new start. As animals, we all let go of our baby teeth partly in order to become an adult. Hanging on to these teeth would cause dental problems, and in this way their surrender is symbolic.

- **Back leg problems and stubborn**, often undiagnosed lameness in a pet can be a sign that in a past life you felt unsupported; this feeling has now tipped over into your current life, perhaps leaving you with a suspicious nature and trust issues which, if left unresolved, can leave you lonely and afraid.

- **Front leg lameness** in your pet means that you find it difficult to reach out to others for help. This overdeveloped sense of independence can mean you push people away. Perhaps you find that friends seem to desert you in your hour of need, when it might actually be you subconsciously putting up barriers they can feel.

- **Back strains** might mean that you find your daily burdens overwhelming and responsibility hard to accept. This can lead to addictions and coming to depend on other unhealthy crutches.

- **Blood diseases** can indicate that in a past life you were emotionally drained and so find commitment to both people and causes in this life difficult. This can make you end up with an unfulfilled life, because you are unlikely to achieve your master plan, what you came here to do, while in this state.

- **Bone diseases** and arthritis can point to you having had family issues in past lives. If your family was dysfunctional in the past, you might not have the right sense of belonging that you should have in this life.

- **Brain illnesses** indicate that in a past life you may have not been listened to or taken notice of. Perhaps you tried to give good advice to someone and he or she refused to listen. It can also show that because of this issue you're lacking in confidence in your own ideas and need to bring your brain power into the open.

- **Breast tumours** in your pet can mean that in past lives you were not nurtured, perhaps by a mother. In this life you need to pamper yourself and trust that your partner loves you – that you are worthy of being loved.

- **Heart complaints** in your pet may show that you faced terrifying circumstances in the past and you either feel subconsciously that you failed to face them adequately, or that you have a heighted sense of danger which can result in many conditions such as OCD (Obsessive Compulsive Disorder) or phobias.

- **Ear problems** can mean that you have a tendency either not to listen to spiritual and/or human companions, or that you listen too hard to whispers and gossip and so become doubtful and mistrusting of friends and partners unnecessarily.

- **If your pet has constant eye problems**, he or she may be trying to bring your attention to the fact that you need to look deeper within yourself and understand why you may have acted the way you have in past lives. This is often associated with feelings of guilt as a result of those actions.

- **If your pet's paws are a worry**, then maybe you need to stand more firmly on your feet and not 'float' away in self-indulgence, or may have needed to do so in a past life. This can affect you by either making you lose touch with reality in this life, or by being so grounded that you've lost all connection to your spiritual side.

- **Mouth problems** would indicate a need to speak out, either now, as a consequence of a past-life event, or in the more recent past. It can also indicate a need for you to understand the power of words, especially harsh words, and how another person's life can be changed by your words.

- **If your pet has bad nail problems**, then this can mean you are being over-defensive in your life. Perhaps you are protecting yourself from people your subconscious recognizes from a past life, when this time around you should forgive them and give them the benefit of the doubt.

- **Skin diseases** can mean that you are not daring to really live, that past-life events haunt you to the extent that you're afraid to let your real self out, for fear that you might get hurt.

THE RESOLVING DOOR

Once you've considered these options, the time has come to help your pet and help yourself at the same time! You must go back to the past-life event that has caused your problems and created the need for your pet to prompt you about it.

The key to this sort of regression is that, whether you do it alone in meditation or with a therapist guiding you into hypnosis, you need to have your pet with you. There are various animal communicators out there who will help you, even with big animals such as horses. I have listed some in the Resources section, but the UK's leading expert in rewriting the script with your pet is Madeleine Walker.

Meditation is, of course, one of the most basic ways to recall past lives. If you're not already skilled at this, then taking some classes would be a good idea to get yourself going. A lot of Buddhist centres offer classes, as do self-help centres. Once you are skilled at meditating, don't worry about your pet. Your calm energy will travel into him and he will easily be able to follow you into the past – or, in some cases, he'll even lead you there. I find that what works best for me and for my clients is to visualize going down a long series of staircases. At the bottom you need to see a row of doors and choose whichever one seems right to you. If you can't choose, ask your pet to choose for you by showing you, in your mind's eye, which door to open.

Things usually happen quite quickly after that. It doesn't matter if your pet links with you and shows you the past, or you recall it for yourself; the important thing is that your path to your current problems will be revealed to you. Once this has happened, you can resolve the issues by simply seeing/re-recording the script with a different outcome. For instance, if you have a phobia of heights, and your pet has been trying to flag up the cause of this by having a heart complaint, you may find that in a past life you and your pet fell or leapt from a high cliff-top to escape some enemies. If this were the case, you could rewrite this script by devising a different outcome, with a different means of escape. Perhaps some allies could come to your rescue, or perhaps the enemies could be distracted and give you a chance to escape another way. Your imagination (your higher self) will be only too happy to devise multiple scenarios once it is given the opportunity.

Bear in mind that it may be too late to save your pet if the condition she suffers from is terminal, but in the big picture this won't matter to her because she will have achieved what she came here for. Don't be too upset or feel guilty, because in the bigger picture you will be together through it and after it and out the other side.

When you start to see the lengths to which our pets are prepared to go in order to help us, their often 'hapless' owners, you come to realize how ridiculous it would be for us to say that they don't have souls. In many ways, animals are truly our spiritual leaders.

HEALING THE RIFT

Here's a heart-warming example of time travelling with your pet and the results it can achieve if conventional medicine hasn't found a cause or cure. It's June's story.

I knew that I needed to look into my past life with my cat, Jessie, because every Christmas, without fail, Jessie would become sick. I know what you're thinking – that it was food treats that caused the problem – but it wasn't. She'd be very ill, vomiting so much that I thought she would die, and one year I was so worried that I took her off to a holiday cottage where there'd be just the two of us, and I know it sounds mad but we just didn't do Christmas. Still, there she was on Boxing Day, as sick as the proverbial parrot. After it was over she'd sleep for hours, unmoving. I lost count of the emergency vet call-outs I had to pay for, but all to no avail: they could never find anything wrong – no fur balls, no fish bones, no infections, no parasites – nothing.

When I followed advice and sat with Jessie to see if I could figure out what was going on, I found our past life came through easily. It took place in the 1600s. Jessie showed me that back then she was a sandy-coloured mongrel dog named Charlie, the best friend of a young boy named Nicholas (me!). This made some sense, as Jessie had always got along surprisingly well with dogs of all kinds and none ever chased her. Anyway, it was the time of the Great Plague and in London, where we lived, it was rife. People were shut up in their houses and left to die if they were thought to be infected. The main symptom was uncontrollable vomiting. It happened to my family one 25 December, and the men came to hammer planks over the doors so that we wouldn't spread the disease. I was terrified that my dog Charlie would die with us. I didn't know if dogs could get the plague or not, but I knew he'd die if he was shut in with us, so at the last second I bundled him out of the door and he was barricaded outside. I thought he'd wander off and find a new home, but it was a huge mistake. He sat outside and cried and howled. It was worse than dying, hearing his distress. Eventually, all my family died, except me, and when I staggered out into the light three weeks later, having been released, I was greeted by the awful sight of poor Charlie's pathetic little body lying on the doorstep. People told me he'd never moved from that spot. Some kind souls said they tried to feed him, but the poor little chap growled when they came near. I expect he thought he was defending me. Of course by the time he was too weak to stop doing that, it was too late to save him. My Jessie was now being sick in an attempt to remind me of our past together and the fact that it needed healing.

I was instructed in how to rewrite this sad tale, so that I could change the past without harming anyone else's, because I knew that Nicholas never actually got the plague. I sat and made a 'video' in my head of the day the door was locked shut, only this time I squeezed out and ran off with Charlie, so the two of us were never parted.

People might say this is just imagination, but placebos don't work on animals and from that day Jessie was never sick again, so make what you will of that!

It's wise when carrying out this method of healing to do it under the supervision of an expert, of which there are several listed on my website, because sometimes there can be dramatic physical results which can be alarming if you're not used to them. Madeleine told me of one incident when she was 'rewriting the script' of a huge horse and his owner. At a pivotal moment both horse and owner collapsed to the floor, which could have caused difficulties if Madeleine hadn't been on hand.

CHAPTER 11

Starting Out Right

If you're unsure of where to look for your compatible pet soulmate, numerology and other modalities can help you make the best start

A life lived without animals would be like a world covered in desert, uninteresting and unsustainable.

– JENNY SMEDLEY

If you've had a very special bond with a pet, then I'm sure you can empathize and perhaps take comfort from the stories in this book. If you've never formed that bond, and maybe have even tried a few times with a few animals and not found one with whom you connect, but would love to, then I may be able to help you.

When choosing a pet, the first thing is to make sure that you're compatible. A few people have argued that surely 'pets choose us'. Well, it won't make any difference who's doing the choosing, the key is to use whatever means to bring the two parties together. One of the methods I've found works very well with pairing people and pets is the tool of numerology. It won't matter who is directing the 'cast' – a supreme being, the universe, the animal or the would-be pet owner – the key is to find a tool that works for any of the parties to manipulate.

I've just concentrated here on the 'small animal' aspect because if someone's never had a successful owner/pet relationship, he or she would be well advised to start with something small and relatively controllable, and in any case animals who are meant to be with us can choose to inhabit whatever body is suitable.

First of all let me explain a little about the art of numbers. Numerology was invented by Pythagoras, and most scientists believe that the cosmos runs on numbers and that any message can be translated into a universally understood language, if numbers are used. So how does it work?

First you need your own date of birth – then, to find your personality number, you add just the first two numbers. For example, if your date of birth is the 29th, 2 + 9

= 11, and 1 + 1 = 2, so there is a personality number of 2. If your date of birth is the 14th then 1 + 4 = 5, so your personality number would be 5.

Next you need to know what this number means, so that you can pair up with a pet who won't have a personality clash with you.

ONE

A very positive person. Self-confident with a strong sense of adventure.

Obviously in this case you need a pet who would enjoy long hill-walks; challenging experiences, such as dog agility, would suit you both. However, beware if you want a dog in one of the more aggressive breeds (such as Dobermann or Rottweiler), as there could be a battle for position of 'pack leader'. On the other hand, you wouldn't want a pet who needs a lot of pampering as you are rather independent and would like your pet to be the same. My top tip would be a Springer Spaniel or Border Collie if you want to win at dog agility. Steer clear of long-haired breeds, as they would require too much grooming.

TWO

If this is your number, you want a pet to talk to and to cuddle. You wouldn't mind a naughty pet because you are very laid-back. My top tip would be a Ragdoll cat. Another choice would be a rabbit or guinea pig, but it would have to be a passive example of the species. On the other hand, you can be a bit moody and won't always be in the mood for 'walkies', so you should stay away from Border Collies, who would resent being ignored and not exercised for whatever reason, and fish, which require a lot more regular attention than people realize.

THREE

Bright, intelligent and fun-loving, you want a pet with whom to share the outdoors, and will always enjoy some rough and tumble. My top tip would be a Boxer dog. On the other hand, Threes can be a bit messy and disorganized, so you wouldn't want a sensitive pet such as a Siamese cat. Not many people make really suitable owners for the very mischievous and sometimes difficult to train Beagle, but you would be one of them.

FOUR

Fours like routine. In fact, Virgos are often Fours. They make loyal friends, too, and once committed to something they're very determined, so they make the perfect pet owner in many respects. On the other hand, they don't like mess, so they need a graceful, low-maintenance dog who doesn't shed, such as a Poodle, or a Cornish Rex cat. Fours should stay away from any animal likely to track too much dirt in, so no pot-bellied or micro pigs for them!

FIVE

An opportunist and someone likely to calmly accept your destiny, you can cope with a pet that others might find a bit neurotic. Outside or indoors, you can handle almost anything that shares your sense of joy in life. You would enjoy a garden full of geese or a timid Pekingese dog. You're capable of calming a frenetic Yorkshire Terrier or re-homing a stressed-out parrot. Even high-energy pets find a soulmate with a Five, so your are the ideal owner to visit the RSPCA or any animal welfare group and to take to your heart an unwanted animal.

SIX

Sixes are often house-proud, so don't like too much mess, but on the other hand they love to be part of a pack and don't care to spend too much time alone. Strangely, they often make good psychologists as they love to know what makes others 'tick'. For these reasons they're unlikely to just have one pet, so they can only really have dogs if they have a large house. If they had a decent-sized garden, they'd enjoy homing several chickens, liking both the practicality of caring for an animal that produces food and also because with chickens they can experience the ultimate 'pecking order' way of living.

SEVEN

Highly imaginative, creative, fastidious and introspective, Sevens are totally 'cat people'. They like a pet who will sit for hours and contemplate with them, neither upsetting the smooth running of the household nor demanding endless hours of play or exercise at inconvenient times. Sevens should certainly never get a 'working breed' of dog, or they could come unstuck. A Burmese cat would be my top choice for them. Either that or an animal who lives outside the home and can be visited as and when required for sharing some quiet thought. A pet sheep would give off the placid energy they'd thrive on.

EIGHT

Eights are usually smooth business operators and wouldn't want anything to distract them from that. They're born organizers and can cope with complicated pets so long as they can walk away for hours at a time and not worry about getting back in time for any kind of strict routine. An aquarium full of beautiful bright fish would suit them very well. It would give them something to sit and watch while resting from their 'empire' duties and would never want to be petted or groomed. This type of pet's needs would quickly become part of the routine and would never be neglected.

NINE

If you are a Nine you have an enhanced sense of justice and will always, literally, support the 'underdog.' For this reason you wouldn't want a pedigree, valuable, much-sought-after pet. For you, the runt of the litter will always have appeal. You wouldn't judge by appearance and any old bandy-legged, funny-faced reject will have you cooing over it and wanting to help it. You just have to watch your energy because feeling too sorry for another being makes your energy weak, and if you don't watch out you can end up bottom of the pecking order and lowest of the pack, which can be dangerous with a high-energy animal. On the other hand, if the pet has energy that's too low, you could both end up needing therapy! So choose a pet you're sure will keep your energy strong, a pet that's balanced with you. Don't just succumb to the sympathy vote.

Of course people will say that all this is unnecessary and the right pet will just find a way to you, but not everyone is adept at reading subtle messages and following gentle signposts, so the above is meant to help those who need a more definite route map, or perhaps need to be shown a more scientific way. In the end, yes, the right pet will get there, but using numerology can speed things up and take away the need to interpret signs and signals quite so much, which some people are not right-brained enough to do. I have advice for the right-brained among you further on in this chapter.

LETTING THEM GO

Having a pet in your life is the most enriching experience, but of course the most common pets don't live as long as us, so at some point we'll inevitably reach the other end of the story, the parting. After my first book I had many people write to me who'd lost their beloved pets and just didn't know how to cope with the loss. Most of them were bowed down under a sense of guilt: did I do the right thing? Did she know how much I loved her? Was there anything I could have done differently? So, I'm ending this book with some help on what to do when your pets reach the end of their lives, in order to give yourself the best chance of recovery from this traumatic time.

Quite often with a pet the moment of loss is something we get some time to think about, as it's not usually sudden. We all hope that our pets will quietly slip away, but that isn't often the case, and so we have to cope with possible feelings of guilt at having made the decision to let them go, as well as the grief of our actual loss. One thing to think about is that, unlike humans, when animals become old or infirm they can't while away the hours pleasantly, reading, chatting or watching TV. If a dog can't run and sniff and do other doggy things, she isn't having a good quality of life. If a cat can't wash and preen and hunt, then he isn't a cat any more. We owe it to our pets to spare them the indignities and suffering that come with terminal illness.

If anyone belittles your feelings of grief, take no notice. They just don't understand. It's very hard to lose a pet. A cat, for instance, can be in your life every day for 18 years. This is more than a lot of people see of their family members, so the grief is very real and the loss is very traumatic.

If you have to face that painful moment, and if euthanasia is involved, then try and stay with your pet while he is sent to sleep. If, however, you aren't able to control your grief and pain, it might be kinder to have another person your pet knows stay with him. This is because animals pick up on our emotions, and if we're crying and distraught, they'll also feel anxious, which is the last thing we want. Whether you're able to stay with your pet or not, it's much kinder to have the vet come to your house rather than taking your pet to the vet's.

Pets Are Forever

With a small animal, what will happen is that she will first be administered a sedative. At this point you should hold her and speak to her, close to her ear, reassuring her that there's nothing to fear. If you can do this then you'll mitigate any later feelings of guilt by knowing you truly did all you could do for her. Once your pet is relaxed, she will be given the injection that will stop her heart. It isn't pleasant but is still quite a peaceful thing. Your pet will quite quickly stop breathing. There may be a couple of abortive attempts to start breathing again, but this is natural. By this point your pet will be out of pain and not in any distress.

If possible, keep your pet at home for at least that night. It's surprising afterwards how much better delaying the abrupt departure of the remains will make you feel. Some say that a pet's soul needs three days and nights to detach from the body, and this has caused a lot of extra grief to people who couldn't or didn't keep the remains that long, who feel they made a dreadful mistake. I beg to differ. Having been with animals when they've died, I've been able to see from the attitude of their companions that it usually takes only up to half an hour for them to leave. Some leave instantly. Also, close-bonded pets are literally attached to their owner's souls, so they're never going to 'get lost'.

172

Most local councils in the UK now recognize the need pet owners have at this time and provide cremation and sometimes burial facilities. This is something you need to organize before the euthanasia takes place. If you opt for cremation, you'll have the option of having the ashes returned to you. Either way, you can help to assuage your grief by creating some sort of memorial. When my beloved dog Ace was cremated, I buried her ashes in the garden under a little standard rose tree called, 'Shine On'. That felt very appropriate.

With a large animal such as a horse, the options are fewer. While it's very unpleasant instinctively to think of your horse being shot with a humane bolt, and easier to think of him being drugged to sleep, do consider the nature of the horse. While a vet can use drugs to euthanize a horse, remember that they're prey animals in the wild, so they can get very scared if they feel their strength gradually failing, and sometimes a quick death is kindest for them. The best thing for both parties, if you can bear it, is to hold the lead rope, feed your horse a carrot and, when the shot comes, walk away without looking back.

If children are involved, then this may be their first experience of death, so make sure their feelings and emotions are handled carefully.

Finally, try not to say 'never again'. It's better, as Tennyson said, 'to have loved and lost, than never to have loved at all'. Also, your pets will never feel betrayed if you decide to get another pet. It's not that you're trying to replace them, because you and they know that isn't possible, it's rather because you can't stand the empty space in your heart and your home that losing them has created. That is a compliment, not an insult. There are thousands of animals in the world who have much to offer and prospective owners who would be fulfilled by them. There are thousands of animals out there who have no hope, and there are prospective owners who can give it back to them. Be brave, walk again into the fire of emotional connection, knowing that it will bring pain in the end, and you'll be a better person for it. Not only that, you might be lucky enough to get your old pet back, if you give him that chance by opening your heart to another pet. Even if your old pet doesn't return, it will be his wish that you help another animal if you can.

SPARK OF YOUR SOUL

Many, many people have written to me to say how special their pet was, and some even seem a little embarrassed at the depth of their grief, saying that some people don't seem to understand it. The thing is this: when you have a relationship with these very special dogs, cats or other pets, they can actually be a spark of your soul. This means that they are connected to you on a deep and spiritual level. Not only have you most likely lived other lifetimes together, but when they pass you literally lose a part of your own soul, a part of yourself. No wonder the pain is so intense, so never feel guilty about it or try to suppress it to suit other people who've never experienced what you're going through. The good news is that, since you are connected on such a deep level, in fact you are never really parted at all; it just feels that way to your mortal self. These animals will almost always stay around you in spirit, and if you open your mind to the little clues, you'll have plenty of evidence of it. Also, they will most likely come back to you in another body, sometimes in this life or sometimes in future lives. So, be comforted. My main fear when I lost my beloved Ace was that being next to me was so important to her in life that I was terrified her spirit would be lost without me, unable to find me and in as much pain without me as I was without her. Of course now I know that was never the case, because her soul is tethered to mine as securely as a boat to its mooring. She could never be lost.

If you've lost this kind of pet you may be wondering how she'll find her way back to you in another body if she's meant to. This can be very hard for pets to do, and occasionally they do fail to make it and have to try yet again when their chosen body passes. This is often because their previous owner either feels too grief-stricken to look for another pet, or is too eager and clutches at the wrong straw. I know people who have done both of these things and so failed to link up with their much loved pet. Animals can only do so much and can only present themselves at the right opportunities. Nothing is set in concrete and mistakes can be made. They will get back to you in the end, but there are ways to avoid such long, drawn-out misery. Some people decide that any animal of the same species and breed, with the same colouring will provide a suitable vehicle for their long-lost pet's soul to inhabit. But it doesn't work that way; animals aren't some kind of alien that can take over another existing body, or even reincarnate into one at their owner's behest.

There was once a so-called psychic who trawled the internet saying that she and only she could direct your old pet's soul into an existing body and thus bring it back to you, and if you didn't consult her then you were likely to lose your pet forever. This struck me as being terribly wrong on many counts. First, no one but the Creator and the animal's soul angel can find the right body to suit that soul's progress. Secondly, what of the soul already inhabiting that body, or due to inhabit that body? That soul has rights, too! To just wildly clutch at a new dog or cat which physically resembles your lost pet can bring heartache and a discontented partnership for both parties.

So, if you believe and hope that your pet is trying to return to you, don't push. Have patience and be vigilant, and the signs will come. These signs are often subtle, but communicate with your passed-over pet in meditation and ask for clues and names to bring you together. If you're unable to do this then go to a proven animal communicator (I have listed some really good ones in the next chapter and in the Resources section) and ask them to bring you the clues you need to rediscover your pet. Sometimes your pet will direct you to a new animal entirely, for instance one whose age doesn't make it possible for him to be carrying the soul of your passed-over pet, and if this turns out to be the case, then trust that your animal spark knows what's best both for you and the animal to which it has taken you.

Trust is a large part of the process of animal and human partnership. Sometimes your pet may be going to reincarnate into a human body, but may want to instigate a new animal partnership for you all the same. Trust is required, but once you accept the premise that you and your beloved pet are united, are joined at a soul level, then this sort of trust becomes easier. Trust me on one thing: the pet you grieve for, and feel you can't live without, will never really leave you. The connection may take a different shape from the comfort of a silky or scaly back, the snuffling sound of love from a furry friend, or the swoop of wings over your head. It may instead take the form of a much-remembered scent, of the weight of an unseen dog on your bed, or the flick of a shadow of a cat's tail passing through a door, but your pet *will* be there, by your side, forever.

CHAPTER 12
Expert Help

Advice on where to go for help if you're unable to make your own connection with your pet

I've interviewed some great animal communicators and healers so that those readers who are unable to make the connection and communicate with their pets by themselves will have an idea of whom to call on for help and for teaching. There's nothing worse than struggling on feeling alone, and there's no need to with great people like these to call on. It will also help to see that even people who are experts today didn't start off that way and that everyone can learn to communicate with their pet. Please write to me and let me know how you get on.

As a child growing up, I loved animals and one of my dearest desires was to be among horses. I can always remember my mother warning me not to go up to strange dogs because they may not be very nice, but that thought had never crossed my mind, and I felt compelled to say hello and make a connection.

On reflection, what my mother was doing was protecting me from harm, but on a deeper level she was imposing her fears upon me – fears that I had not felt, for my connection with the animals was one that my mother was not experiencing. She was having her own experience. This was a learning curve for me: to trust in my own instincts and to believe in myself. What I am feeling, sensing and thinking may not be the same as others but it does not mean I am wrong. I quickly learned that people unintentionally impose unnecessary fears and restrict that intuitive spontaneity we all have as children.

During my childhood I grew up in a family that liked the idea of animals, but never truly embraced what really having animals was meant to be like. So pets very much had their place and lived within some very unsuitable environments, although they were much loved. There was Bruce, who was a Toy Poodle. Bruce was a snappy little thing and for this reason it was felt that he needed a home without children one on one, so we lost him to a new home. Then a journey to Battersea Dogs Home brought Prince into our lives. He was a Welsh Border Collie and, unbeknownst to my parents, an animal that needed a lot of exercise and time in grooming, and with our family's busy lifestyle the true bond of animals and owners never really happened. Prince told us in the only way he knew how that he was unhappy, by leaving his mark in the kitchen where he was kept. But I remember Prince as being happiest when we were very active at the park going down the slides and jumping onto the roundabout.

He had so much love to give but none of us knew how to listen. Then there were several cats that passed through, including Sooty – as you can already imagine, a black tom cat. He was quite big with a flick of white under his chin, and if there was an old cat soul in existence, then that would be Sooty. He seemed to know when we were coming home and was always there to greet each and every one of us. This was just one thing that was most lovable about him. He was such a social, healing animal and he gave pleasure to so many patients at the doctor's surgery that eventually he became the surgery cat, until he passed over at the age of 18.

Many events took place, just as in most people's lives: getting married, having a son, separation from husband and subsequent divorce, before another pet arrived.

When my son was aged three, I felt it was important to introduce him to keeping animals and see the care that was really needed. By this time I knew a lot about handling and caring for animals, and had learned from my family's early mistakes. I'd come to understand the bond there should be between a pet and its owner. I felt it was very important to pass this knowledge on to my son so that he too would love animals as I did and understand that sense of being at one with them.

My son and I chose a little kitten together, but sadly it died within a week, of feline enteritis. This was at least an example to my son of the irresponsibility of some humans. If people are going to allow their cats to mate then they should make sure they are safe to mate. The tragedy of the kitten's death happened one night while I was at work, and my son had been collected from the day nursery by his granddad. As they walked into the kitchen they discovered the little one already in a very poor state.

In time we gave a home to two black kittens and chose to call them Bonnie and Clyde. Clyde was such a big cat and an adventurer, always out exploring, but one night he never came home and from that moment Bonnie was never far from sight. She was almost a house cat, but she was quite dominant, knowing how to let my son know when he'd gone too far, but it was always only just enough to let him know. She had a heart of gold that gave unlimited love and affection as well as laughter. You would find her sleeping in the oddest of places and the smallest of containers, wrapped around the top of a plant pot or tucked in a toy box. Her typing skills on the computer far exceeded my own, and to write with a pen was just fun. I could almost hear her laughter as she frustrated my progress; what a delight to know that personality and have those memories now of all our much loved pets.

Shortly after my father passed, and by the time my son was 14, a little Maltese Terrier came into our lives, and we called her Pepper. She was funny and so little – this ball of white fluff that could squeeze under furniture and followed you everywhere. Pepper was like the little girl I had never had. She brought immeasurable joy, and as the bond between us grew, the trust was without question. She knew that if I told her something, it was for her own good, and she responded as if she knew what every word meant. So often she'd know what I was doing before I knew what I was doing, and her patience and loyalty were immeasurable. She played often with her sister, who lived nearby, going for walks and runs, barking for play, to warn and for attention. Her sister used to tell tales on her. Pepper was a laid-back, relaxed, cool-dude type of dog and her sister was highly strung and somewhat constipated with stress. If Pepper, for whatever reason, couldn't get out of the door, her sister used to go up to her owner and pull on her leg until she followed her downstairs, or from the other side of the house, to let her know that the door wasn't opened for Pepper and that she hadn't been able to hold it. Together they were amazing and brought tears of joy to us so often. As I remember this now, the tears touch my eyes for the loss of that most beautiful of friendships, based on love, loyalty and trust. Pepper may have been stuck in a four-legged body, but she was as human as you and me, with eyes that you became lost in as the love shone through.

Our life together was a 13-year betrothal of constant companionship and togetherness. She passed on 18 February 2007. Early that Sunday morning it was a day like any other. There were no signs that she was leaving me that day, none at all – quite the opposite, for I knew when she was not well and there were no signs. Almost to the day the previous year, Pepper had became very ill and I'd had to take her to the vet's, asking them to tell me what was wrong with her, but none of what they did seemed to help – in fact, the medication made her worse. So I took my faith and belief in myself and stopped all medications and began to treat her naturally through vitamins and diet, and the minute I did so she seemed to rally. I researched foods and supplements, finding out what she needed to maintain a balanced and healthy life with all the necessary nutrients. Only occasionally did she taste pre-packed or manufactured food again. She enjoyed such a variety of breakfasts and dinners, and ate as well as any human. It kept her going for another year – a year for which I would be forever grateful because that last year together was possibly the most connected one could ever hope for.

Pepper was a teacher in my life in many ways, and she still remains so in the spirit world. It was she who laid the ground-breaking knowledge in me that we can actually communicate with animals, and this is what I in turn try to pass on today. However, the shock of her going was enough to bear for a few days. I lit a candle for her and laid her to rest in her bed, which she'd loved dearly. I rang her sister's mum, and of course my son, so they could say goodbye. It was the weekend so it felt reasonable to keep her body until the following Tuesday, making Monday the time to make arrangements and prepare her physical body. This enabled her soul the time to transit into the spirit world. Her passing was so sudden it felt right to allow time and space as we know it.

It turned out that Pepper had passed of an aneurysm, which is a small clot of blood, and within seconds she was gone. If there were any one way to pass from this life to another, this would have to be one of the kindest ways. After Tuesday, it was so quiet. All normality had been disrupted. There were no demands like feeding and walking Pepper, no food to prepare, no doors to open, no friend by my side, and the tears flowed slowly as I tried to understand – why? Why was it so important for Pepper to leave now? When I asked the question in my mind, the answer came that I had always put her first and it was now my time to put myself first and move forward in life. Here was my Pepper talking with me from the spirit world, and as usual she was so right. Life had become very restricted, working and breathing life from home. When we did go out, she was the first to be said hello to, followed by me; when we walked, she was first to greet all people and the first to warn me of bad people. In some ways she knew that she stood between me and the outside world, and she continues to guide me and comfort me. When I teach, she teaches with me and has become the most natural animal to communicate with and learn from. I know now that I have not lost her because she walks within me and with me wherever my path leads, and she is still leading – no one else sees her, that's all. But I believe, and that's all that matters.

Teaching animal communication to others is when we work together most, to bring about the tremendous rewards and realizations, so that people can experience that same belief for themselves. I want to teach that we can all communicate with animals without exception. Our faith and willingness to believe it is possible are the key. The workshops I run are aimed at providing people with this knowing and belief in themselves that they too can communicate with animals without question. They come to know that with practice they can develop the skill to truly engage with the animal with which they're communicating, which can then provide healing on many levels. I'm able to have a three-way conversation with owner and the animal, with myself as the pivotal connector, and aim to teach this to others. I am also able to teach people to locate an animal that is lost, remembering that it's only lost as far as the owner's concerned, and it's not until you communicate with the animal that you can know if they are truly lost or have just left home by choice. Animal communication is an opportunity to relate to the animals' world and understand their mental, physical, emotional and spiritual being; what it is they want from us – what their purpose is in our lives. It's when we see the balance of control in this way that we are able to truly touch the soul of an animal as an equal.

Linda Lowey

www.talkingwithanimals.co.uk

You might wonder, if you ask me to do a healing session on your pet, what you'll be expected to do, if anything. The answer is: very little. During a distant healing session with me, your pet can be allowed to do whatever they want because I'll be working on their energy field, and their physical place in space won't impact on that.

During a hands-on healing session, your pet may investigate my hands or push their body into my hands, or stay away from me and observe me. There are no rules; your pet will be in charge of the session and I'll work with them with my hands on their body or just with them, even if they're sitting away from me. Your pet might go into a deep state of relaxation or even sleep. Be assured that all animals are treated with love, compassion and respect.

As an animal communicator and healer, I often come across animals that are aware that they're on the last leg of their journey on Earth, animals that have a mission in this life, and animals requesting to be helped to pass over. These are just some of the stories of these amazing animals.

One communication I did a few years ago, with a cat called Barnaby, illustrates how much animals are aware of their own mortality and the purpose of their lives.

Barnaby's guardian contacted me, as she wanted to know how he was feeling. After a little chit-chat about him, his life, his favourite activities, food, etc., he then conveyed to me as a matter of fact that his time on Earth was coming to an end. He simply made me aware of that fact, without drama and without fuss. To me he was a kind of Bob Marley of the feline world: cool and laid-back. He was very chilled out about an event he knew was coming. The wisdom and acceptance emanating from him were mind-blowing, and I could not believe my ears. It was highly unexpected to have an animal telling an animal communicator about their imminent passing without being prompted. He just dropped it in the conversation, as you do.

He explained to me that he was quite ready to undertake his last journey, that he had had a wonderful and exciting life with his guardian and that his body was growing old and weary. At this point Barnaby was in good health, with only a problem with his gums. The vet had found nothing wrong with him and he was enjoying a good life, being mischievous and arguing with his sister, a fiery ginger cat.

Five months later, his guardian contacted me again as she was worried that he was declining but the vet couldn't find anything wrong with him. As soon as I connected with Barnaby, I could feel that his energies were running low and that indeed his life-force was slowly decreasing.

He was happy to communicate with me and told me that the end was drawing closer.

He told me that his purpose in life had been to look after his guardian and to make her unwind. This made me smile, as his guardian is someone who's always on the go, very busy and sociable, and rarely quiet and relaxed. He made sure she took some time to stroke him or to play with him; he greeted her when she came back home; he slept on her bed and her pillow to be close to her. In all, he was her little shadow. To him his mission was simple but powerful and he felt he'd accomplished it. Again, serenity and peace were all around him, and he was very philosophical about his own demise. He conveyed that he would go on his own when the final hour was upon him, and little did I know what he really meant by that.

A few months later his guardian contacted me again, and I could sense in her voice that something was wrong. Barnaby had disappeared without trace. Baffled, I communicated with Barnaby straight away, and the answers came back clear to me. Barnaby had gone somewhere reclusive to inhale his last breath on Earth. His body was somewhere in the neighbourhood, but his soul had ascended and was long gone from his forlorn body. He gave me a specific message for his guardian, and expressed that his passing was peaceful and as he had wanted. His guardian received the message with a heavy heart and said she'd known in her heart that he was gone. I'll never forget this communication, as it made me understand that some animals have psychic abilities and know about their own future and are very conscious of their mortality.

Another extraordinary and remarkable story about the soul of an animal is the following.

I was asked to do some healing sessions on a wonderful little dog called Zephyr. She was a very cute little madam who had a problem with breathing. Often during healing, I leave the communication channel open to let the animal commune with me if they want to. Zephyr knew that and took advantage of the offer. She conveyed a few things about what had been done to her sleeping arrangements in recent times and displayed her disapproval. When I told her guardian about this, the woman was stunned by Zephyr's request, which made loads of sense. She put the original arrangements back and, hey presto, Zephyr displayed her satisfaction.

The healing sessions went well and Zephyr's breathing problem started to abate, and even disappeared altogether. She asked for a few things to be given to her to improve her health (she was in her twilight years). She improved very much after a few simple adjustments to her diet, and she enjoyed her walks and life.

A few months after the healing, her guardian contacted me and told me that Zephyr had passed away unexpectedly in their garden. The woman was inconsolable and I must admit I, too, was sobbing on the telephone, as this little dog had so much charisma and character. I was very fond of her.

A few days later, the woman phoned again and told me that Zephyr had appeared to her in the front room, her body restored to full health, her coat shining, looking like a young dog again. The apparition lasted for a few minutes and the woman said that Zephyr told her not to grieve for her as she was happy now and that soon enough she'd be back on Earth. The woman was very happy to have seen her dog one last time and she wanted my opinion on the matter. I told her that I believed she indeed saw her dog and that possibly another puppy would come into her life very soon that would remind her of Zephyr. Sure enough, two months later the woman contacted me again and told me that she'd adopted a new puppy. She sent me some photos for me to have a look at and I could feel Zephyr's spirit around this puppy. The woman confirmed that the new puppy displayed loads of the character traits and likes and dislikes that Zephyr had had.

I found this curious, as they were not the same breed at all, so these similarities could not be classified as breed characteristics. Very strange indeed, but I am happy to know that Zephyr is now happy somewhere in the Rainbow Bridge and perhaps her soul has already found love with her guardian in a new body.

My own story with my animals reflects that sometimes animals ask to be helped to pass over.

I used to have an African pygmy hedgehog called Zoe. She was an adorable companion, full of character and mischief, very aware of her own mind and very determined, too. We had five blissful years together. The last few months of her life were the most difficult and yet the most powerful time I have had with an animal. She was diagnosed with wobbly hedgehog syndrome, which despite the funny name is a serious condition leading to death. It is often compared to multiple sclerosis in humans.

As an animal healer, I knew that some complementary therapies could help to alleviate Zoe's pain and help her emotionally with the debilitating symptoms she soon had, such as incontinence, a wobbly walk and pain. For months I hid my feelings and emotions and I dedicated myself to her wellbeing, doing hydrotherapy, physiotherapy, hands-on and distant healing, giving her the most natural diet I could think of, treating her with flower remedies for her wellbeing, together with conventional veterinary treatment. Zoe seemed to cope well and she often told me that she was grateful for my help – that was, until one day while I was doing a healing session and I heard clear and loud in my mind that I should stop doing healing because it wasn't required any longer. In that moment I knew she was going to be released from her earthly body. Sure enough, it happened a few weeks later.

On the morning of Zoe's passing, I found her dishevelled in her box and thoughts came straight away in my mind: 'It's time for me to go, let me go please. I need help to leave this body.' With tears rolling down my cheeks, I made an emergency appointment with the vet. During the whole journey to the surgery Zoe lay on my arm, her little nose resting against my armpit and her eyes locked into mine. I could hear her clearly telling me that she'd had a good life, that she was grateful for all that we'd done for her and that her time had come. She was in loads of pain and wanted to go, and wanted it all to stop. The vet confirmed our worst fears. There was a massive tumour on Zoe's stomach, and I had to say my final goodbyes to my little soulmate.

She was put to sleep on the spot and I'll never forget touching her little face and talking sweetly to her while tears cascaded down my cheeks. Zoe looked at me and made a big effort to lift her head, and she telepathically said thank you to me. Then she was at peace and I knew her next adventure would begin.

I since have adopted two Persians rescue cats, and one of them was born the same year as Zoe passed, and some of the things he does remind me of her. Could it be that she has found her way home again? Perhaps it is wishful thinking, but deep inside I do believe she hasn't left us. She's somewhere around us, and she's definitively in our hearts.

Oephebia

www.animalscantalk2me.com

I've been a professional animal communicator since 2000, serving clients throughout my home state of Illinois, in other parts of the Midwest and across the USA. My desire to assist animals and their human companions is inspired by my feline companion, Panda, a graceful, wise and playful friend, who passed into spirit when my journey on this path began.

In the autumn of 1999, Panda went into sudden kidney failure. I was devastated and emotional. At the time I knew someone who had the capability to communicate the thoughts and feelings of animals. This counsellor let me know Panda's thoughts about what I was doing to assist her, and it helped us both through a very difficult six-week period. Near the end of Panda's life, I began to pick up her thoughts myself. It was a total joy for us both to have this connection.

When the time came to help Panda with her physical passing, this heart-to-heart and mind-to-mind connection made the experience one of understanding and discovery, rather than of complete sorrow. It was a wonderful gift. At that point I received the confirmation that this connection with animals and Nature was part of my life purpose, along with helping others to connect with their animal companions in the same way.

Following these profound experiences and realizations, I transitioned into working more closely with animals. I became a veterinary assistant with a local animal rehabilitation clinic, a pet-sitter and also a volunteer at animal sanctuaries.

Early on in my journey as an animal communicator, I began facilitating courses to help others regain their telepathic ability and confidence to communicate with animals. My passion to educate and support others who desire a deeper connection with their own companions has resulted in thousands of students participating in these courses. I'm very honoured to have now numerous professional animal communicators and holistic animal healers as my peers, who began their path as students seeking this both magical and scientific connection with their companions.

My commitment to deep emotional healing of both animals and their people drove my desire to found the Animal Spirit Healing & Education® Network. Launched in 2006, ASN is a collaborative educational platform dedicated to enhancing the lives of animal companions and their humans. This vision is offered through on-site courses, teleclasses and online learning opportunities in areas of animal wellness.

I live in Pekin, Illinois, with my daughter and two cats, Augie and Blinky, and I'm a full-time animal communicator and director of Animal Spirit Network.

Here is just one example of a response from a client:

Thank you so much for the kind email and especially for the communication last night. I could not possibly put into words what it meant to me, and how much I admire your gift. It is truly a gift of healing and quite obviously directly from God. This type of work seems to me to be sacred and necessary. We discover how profound the connections are between all beings, particularly those we live with, and how meaningful those connections are. It was also obvious to me how much the animals trusted you; they gave you so much and so quickly. You were absolutely correct about their different personalities and energies. Thank you again. You are on the path to extraordinary things! I am glad to walk part of the way with you.

– With great love from Joanne, Amber,

Little Cat and Deva

In my work with clients I've found that the animals and I work best in a question-and-answer format. Generally it's most effective if the client plans in advance what questions they'd like to directly ask their companion(s) during a consultation session. This helps the session to be grounded and productive for all participating. A suggested range of six to nine questions for one animal works very well for most cases, and we allow time during the session flow for additional questions and topics to be incorporated based on the responses.

Most animals have a very deep desire to communicate and are looking forward to discussing numerous topics they've been waiting to share. By planning ahead, it's helpful to ensure that the key items at this time are covered during the session. The client's companion will also have many opportunities to share additional topics and thoughts throughout the connection and time together.

The animal's name, breed/physical description, gender and age are needed for the session. Pictures are not necessary, but if the session is by phone, it's helpful to have a picture for the consultation and for future use if additional conversations become scheduled.

During the communication session I always prefer to let the animal talk first before continuing with the prepared questions. This provides the client's companion with the opportunity to relay what they'd like to at the beginning. The translation is sentence by sentence, so the client receives the translation almost as soon as the animal provides the response.

Miracles and Surprises

Remaining open to surprises and profound healings, I have noticed that sometimes the smallest nuances can be the cosmic key that unlocks an area of healing for both the animal and person. Trust turned that key in one of my very first cases.

Duke the cat greeted me telepathically by barking at the beginning of a client phone session. I reconnected telepathically several times, thinking that possibly my next canine client was arriving early to connect, but I kept receiving the same response: barking. I stepped back telepathically and checked in with myself again to ensure I was grounded and neutral, and yet the barking continued. Trusting, I addressed the barking as Duke, the feline. The door of telepathic communication opened, and Duke, a young personality of much enthusiasm and adventure, came through. He'd wanted to be a dog, which explained some of his unfriendly and frustrating behaviours with other cats in the house.

Acknowledging Duke in this way went a long way toward establishing more harmony in the home, as interactions with other cat family members notably improved following the session.

A large part of my practice is related to clients connecting with animals close to passing on.

One of my clients, Margaret, was struggling with the loss of her long-time canine companion, Lady. She shared stories and pictures with me about their life together, and Lady wanted to share her memories as well! Lady assured Margaret that she was doing well and surrounded by angelic support and nurturing. She described being in a majestic cathedral with gorgeous marble pillars and floors, a place filled with formality and traditions. In conveying this to Margaret, it was clear validation to her that Lady was safe and in a place of spiritual rest. A weight was visibly lifted for them both.

Eventually, Lady returned in a new physical body to enjoy the earthly realm with Margaret once again. There was a period of time before Lady's reincarnation when she indicated that she was coming back as a feline, with an intention to be an easy-to-care-for companion as Margaret enjoyed retirement. However, energies shifted prior to her physical return, and Lady chose to return as a very perky and very active puppy. Margaret was thrilled beyond measure to be reconnected with her dear companion, now named Chloe, and have young and lively energy to brighten her life.

Lost animal cases are another area where I serve clients. There are both difficulties and rewards in supporting someone who is searching for a lost companion. Over the years I have developed an approach that works well for me. I have also found that some students really have a strong talent for lost animal cases, which I encourage to blossom.

For lost animal cases, I typically approach the session as a 20- to 30-minute connection. This provides an opportunity to receive first impressions regarding the potential condition and whereabouts of the lost animal, and convey energetic guidance on how to assist in reconnecting the client with their companion. This process of working with lost animals continuously evolves.

Lost animal cases tend to be accompanied by strong emotional stress factors, so it's important for the animal to sense their person being grounded and centred during the conversation. This will enhance the communication exchange and subsequent search.

In one lost animal case, Boise and Clyde, indoor/outdoor cats, set out on an adventure in the middle of a Chicago winter. Each time I spoke to them they reassured me they were fine, warm enough and finding food. They also said they knew the way home and could get there, but after a couple of conversations it became apparent that they were waiting for something to change at home. Their human caretaker, Joanne, needed to make some changes in her life and, according to Boise and Clyde, their ongoing absence was meant to be the catalyst.

The cats were gone for a chilling three weeks and there was a distinct sign when they were about to return. About 20 to 30 minutes into some serious discussion, I felt a huge shift energetically and actually heard a pop, like opening a vacuum-sealed jar. Conveying this to Joanne, Boise and Clyde communicated that they would now return home, and they concluded the session. I didn't know how long they would be, but lo and behold, the following morning Boise poked into the window left open for his return. He took off again, but shortly thereafter, apparently after

Boise gave Clyde the 'all clear', both cats came trotting in together, as if nothing had happened.

Final Thoughts

My advice to clients and students is to trust your intuition, listen to your heart and spend quiet time with your animals, Nature and yourself. Honour who you are, nurture yourself, let go and have fun.

Animals see your heart, past the things that distract us from our core. Trust the animals as teachers and compassionate reminders of the love and balance that are continuously available when we pause and notice.

Carol Schultz

carolschultz.com

'What on Earth are you doing with that cat?' This was a phrase I would undoubtedly hear almost every day from my parents, from the time when I was aged about eight and my dad brought home a scrawny black semi-feral cat to 'keep me company'. As an only child with extremely busy parents, I would occupy myself by reading anything on the subject of animals. I'd hide myself away in my bedroom and have my nose under a mountain of non-fiction books.

One day Dad, who worked as a builder at a city steelworks, had taken over the task of feeding the foundry cats from his colleague, who'd gone on holiday. All of them were stray cats who had been carelessly cast aside into this harsh, industrial landscape, from homes that perhaps they'd thought would be theirs forever.

A black cat that I later named Timmy had a big impact on my dad. Timmy was semi-feral, and although my dad tried to coax him to eat, his appetite was poor. After hiring a trapping cage, Dad rescued Timmy and brought him home. I was overjoyed to have a companion with whom to share silly moments and secrets. We bonded almost straight away, but after a week we had to take Timmy to see the vet because he was losing weight drastically and his appetite was increasingly poor. After numerous tests over a few days, Timmy was diagnosed with a renal tumour. He was given an injection and a few pills, and we were advised that we should expect Timmy to live no more than three or four months. We were also told that the life Timmy had suffered had most likely contributed to his condition. The vet asked to see Timmy again in another four weeks and that we should decide what we wanted to do. We took Timmy home. I was devastated. How could I allow this little man to suffer? What could I possibly do to help him? I couldn't just leave him to die, could I? Unaware of what I was doing, I placed Timmy in his basket and sat at the side of him, placed my hands upon him and immediately felt immense, almost pulsating energy flow through me. Timmy started to 'heat up and buzz'. It was akin to a light being turned on. Mum looked at me and obviously thought it was such a strange thing to do, but to me it was natural. I held out my hands, lightly touching Timmy's tiny body for around ten minutes, until I saw his expression turn almost serene, and then I stroked him from head to tail.

Each day after school I'd rush in and demonstrate what I now know is healing with Timmy. After about a week Timmy started to pick up, raise his head in interest at food and start to eat, and he even started to play with pieces of string that I'd pull across the floor for him. In fact, he started to behave like a normal, healthy feline! Four weeks passed and upon our visit to the vet, as he prodded and poked my little friend, he had quite a perplexed look upon his face. 'I'd like to run a couple more tests,' he said. With the result of the tests, a rather bemused vet told us that the previously satsuma-sized renal tumour was now the size of a pea. How could this be? The vet said he hadn't seen anything like it, and he couldn't offer us an explanation. Was it the injection at the initial consultation? Was it the two weeks' worth of painkillers? Was it the energy that I had channelled? I honestly can't say and neither could the vet at that time. One thing I do know is that Timmy went on to live another eight years and finally passed to Rainbow Bridge peacefully in his sleep, aged 16!

Prior to us having Timmy, when I was about three or four, I remember Mum telling me that on our way to nursery school she'd be shooing away the cats that would jump off gate posts to follow me. I also remember a time when Mum was late to collect me from school, when I was about nine, and I was waiting at the school gates when all the other children had gone home. Sitting beside me was a Dalmatian, which I later found out was named Jason, and a Border Collie, called Dilly. It was as if the dogs knew Mum would be late and wanted to keep me safe. I was also always the one in my circle of friends to ask to take the neighbours' dogs for a walk rather than to play with dolls.

Upon leaving school I went straight to college to study business and finance, and then went to work within the Social Services. I gained little from my post, and the stress it created led me to have a mild stroke aged just 24. I was on holiday and it was my first wedding anniversary. I refused all medication even though the doctor advised it would be likely that I'd have another stroke within six months. I looked toward holistic methods of healing and recuperation, and I also looked within myself. I did self-healing every day, meditation and visualization, and I also had regular reflexology and Reiki healing treatments. When I'd healed my body and felt stronger within myself, I decided that the stroke was a turning point in my life and I embarked upon a change of career, much to the disappointment of some family members. I trained for the next eight years in various modalities of complementary therapy and in psychological counselling, and I also trained for two years in Reiki healing and became a Reiki Master Teacher. That was 14 years ago.

Throughout my twenties I found my diary divided between animal clients and human ones. I worked with a varying range of species from horses, dogs, cats and other domestic animals to llamas, alpacas, snakes and marmoset monkeys! My name was being passed on by word of mouth far and wide and I found myself travelling throughout the UK to see animals and their human companions. I was called anything from a Spiritual Master, Animal or Kitty Whisperer, Guru, Animal Visionary and even Mrs Doolittle, but really I was just me working doing something that I loved.

Meditation helped me tremendously with my recovery to good health, during which I received great inspirational messages and guidance, telling me that I had to pass on knowledge to others to define and validate the work that I was doing. I needed to express a language of what I was doing from the heart and help others tap into this great energy within themselves. In 1998 I received what can only be called 'an awakening', and I knew that this was the path on which I had to walk.

I knew in my heart that many people wanted to share this deeper bond with their own animals, and indeed the whole of the animal kingdom, and to recognize that they were not separate from these creatures. So for three years I worked devising a professional animal healing training course. Thus, Animal Magic© healing training courses were born. It took another couple of years to have the syllabus assessed for insurance and now my courses are fully insurable for students to become part of this magical world of animal healing. I always say to students that even if you don't wish to work as a full-time animal healer like myself, the course will help you to become a full-time magical person!

On this journey I've had the pleasure of teaching many differing individuals, working in and out of the animal field from horse trainers, veterinary nurses, postgraduate students, rescue centre volunteers and even a woman of 82! I've even had people leaving their jobs within the legal profession and even the police to become full-time animal healers. I'm currently in the process of setting up a healing practice solely for animals – the first of its kind in East Anglia.

I believe that anyone can achieve great things in animal healing. You need not possess a 'gift'; we all have the gift if we just tap into a part of ourselves that has lain dormant for so long. Healing is a re-awakening of mind. It is learning to trust our own spirit and intuition. It is also believing that great things are possible. I have seen some near-miracles since I first helped heal Timmy 30 years ago.

The way I work as a professional is first and foremost to adhere strictly to the code of conduct and ethics in working with animals. I also work within the law of The Veterinary Protection Act, which includes following stringent health and safety guidelines.

Upon an initial visit I go through a detailed consultation form with the animal's guardian, which includes medical history, dates of vet visits and details of the background of the animal, etc. Once I have built a rapport with both owner and animal, I will then connect to the animal by using many methods which can include dowsing, scanning and energy sensing. I then begin to tap into the energy field, demonstrating a variety of hand positions. At any one time I could be using colour, light, sounds, mantras, mudras, healing symbols and intuitive or Reiki healing. When I have observed the body language of my patient, I will end the treatment by grounding the energy within the auric field and go on to share information and intuitive insight with the animal's guardian. It's important to know, however, that I do not diagnose any condition. This post-healing information often opens up great surprises for the animal's guardian, as often the information I interpret is profound and quite moving, since animals communicate with me during their healing on many levels.

It's how the animal responds to the healing itself that will determine how many subsequent visits will be required. As a general guide, normally four to five treatments are enough for physical ailments, but emotional or behavioural problems may take a few more sessions, as often deeper-level healing is needed to resolve deep-rooted thought patterns and negative or self-destructive behaviour.

When I'm working with horses it's often like sharing the same soul. This may sound strange, but equine energy is akin to the energy of the human being – sensitive, intelligent and aware. Horses also respond to our body language and this can have a great impact on their behaviour. More often than not I have treated both owner and horse in the same session, and indeed showed tips on how the guardian can affect the horse's energy field in subtle but profound ways, through their connection with their own horse.

It is important to listen to horses. Equine energy has so much to share with us and to teach us.

A quiet and relaxed mind must be the basis of a deeper connection to our animal companions. Furthermore, any notion that animals are lesser beings must be swept aside. Animals should be nurtured and cared for if we are to share our lives with them.

Animals are no way beneath us. They should not be persecuted in any way or used for monetary gain, or indeed suffer untimely death or be slaughtered for human consumption. If you want to develop a deeper bond, then please think a while on the previous sentence, as it deserves great thought and compassion. Having an animal show unconditional love for us can have a deep effect on our personalities. Cats don't care how we look or if we have put on an extra few pounds. Dogs don't care how untidy the kitchen drawers are, and horses certainly don't care what the latest 'must have' fashion accessory is. Their connection with us is deep and will be everlasting. We can tap into this unconditional love and energy simply by placing our hands upon them, sensing their energy and becoming a part of it. Notice – do you feel heat, or cold, or a tingling sensation? Are you picking up words, images, phrases or lines from songs, as I often do? When making this initial contact it's important not to dismiss these feelings and impressions, as we are working with intuition and not the left, logical and scientific part of the brain. In healing we are working with what our ancestors used for hundreds of years – intention, awareness and belief to bring about positive change on many levels.

I'm truly blessed to be learning and teaching something for which, I believe, I was put on this Earth – to work as a full-time animal healer. Upon my journey I have met with personal struggles, but the blessings far outweigh any adversity. I've met some wonderful souls, both animal and human, who've played a major part in my past, present and also my future life. These thanks go to them. I am forever indebted to that scrawny black semi-feral cat named Timmy, but for whom I wouldn't be living my dream now. Thank you, Timmy, you taught me so much, you shared your heart and soul with me, you are forever my guide.

Niki Senior

www.ukanimalhealer.co.uk

These are the professional animal communicators, but some people, like Tracey, whose story is below, have a natural ability which they just use on a personal and gentle level.

I've always loved animals from as soon as I could walk. I never had any pets of my own until I was at primary school, but my grandparents had dogs and cats. My mum said that when I was a baby she would take me round to see my grandparents and put me down to sleep in their bedroom. If I cried, my granddad's Boxer dog, Caesar, would start barking at my mum until she'd go and make sure that I was all right. Caesar and Sandy, the Golden Labrador, always looked after me as I grew up. They were so gentle and I loved them to bits.

My mum said I was always stroking dogs and cats when I was little, and she was sometime scared as she would turn around and I'd be petting some big dog. My mum said I was lucky I never got bitten. I was never scared of animals and I think I never got bitten because I loved them all and they knew it. I can remember when I was about three or four and we went to Knole Park and I went up to the deer and a big stag and stroked them. I have a picture of me and the stag.

I've had lots of other experiences, but my most interesting took place when I worked at a wildlife rescue centre. I worked there for about two years, helping to feed and clean out cages of the sick wildlife. We used to get lots of birds and fledglings as well. Looking after these animals and birds, I used to get feelings and I'd know if an animal was going to survive or die. My feelings were always right and it was sad when I knew they'd die, but when they were going to live, it was such a great feeling. One very strong experience was when we had a badger cub in the hospital room, only about three months old. It was very poorly. I wasn't looking after it, as badgers have to be looked after by only one person otherwise they will get overly imprinted with people. I was told by another carer that it wasn't drinking or eating and they didn't think it would live the night. When I was the only person in the hospital room, I knelt down to the badger cub in its open pen and started to talk to it and it slowly came over to me. It looked poorly and I dipped my hand into its water bowl. It came over to my hand and licked it and then took a small amount to drink from its bowl. I told the badger,

'You poor thing. You must get better.'

That night as I slept at home, I was suddenly woken from my sleep. I had a warm but also sick feeling in my stomach. I knew the badger was at crisis point. I said, 'Please be OK,' and then I went back to sleep. In the morning I woke up wondering if the badger was alive. I got into work and went straight into the hospital room. My boss was there and she said that she was so pleased the badger cub was better. She couldn't believe it as she'd been so sure that it wouldn't be strong enough to survive the night. I was really happy, too, although I didn't tell anyone about what happened to me that night or my other feelings with the sick animals. I'm 38 years old now and I am mad about cats. I have two Burmese cats that I love to bits.

Afterword

My final advice is, if you want to get closer to your pets, first of all make sure you allow time in your schedule for some quiet moments alone with them. It's all too easy in our rat-race lives to only just about fit in the chores our pets create for us — cleaning out, grooming, feeding, etc. Always remember that energy travels, and if your energy is always hectic around your animal friends, then they won't really be in the right frame of mind to connect with you on a deep level. Animals, in general, and certainly most small animals, don't live very long in relation to humans — not in one life anyway — and the years will pass in a flash, so don't waste any of it. Just find time occasionally to sit quietly and ask your pet questions in your mind when it's still enough. Then be receptive to a response. If you start off by asking small things that can be verified, such as 'Do you want to get your ball?' or 'Do you want to get a drink?' and your pet seems to say, 'Yes,' then release her with a thought and see if she goes and does what you suggested.

The next step would be to ask your pet what he wants to do and see if you get an answer. If you do, then again release him and see if he does what you were thinking about. Some pets work in colour – even though people will tell you that they don't all see in colour – and if, for instance, you ask them if they're in pain, they might show you the colour red for yes and the colour green for no. Start simple … and build. Explore your pet's way of thinking and develop your own language. Before long you'll be having proper conversations with your pet.

Recommended Reading

Allen and Linda Anderson, *Angel Dogs* (Penguin, 2009)

Paul Gallico, *Thomasina* (Penguin, 1964)

Jenny Smedley, *Forever Faithful* (O Books, 2009)

Jenny Smedley, *Pets Have Souls Too* (Hay House, 2009)

Jackie Weaver, *Animal Talking Tales* (Local Legend Publishing, 2010)

Madeleine Walker, *The Whale Whisperer* (Findhorn Press, 2011)

Resources

I've been given permission by Penelope Smith to include here her code of ethics, by which in my opinion all animal communicators should be bound:

CODE OF ETHICS FOR INTERSPECIES TELEPATHIC COMMUNICATORS

Formulated in 1990 by Penelope Smith,
www.animaltalk.net

Our motivation is compassion for all beings and a desire to help all species understand each other better, particularly to help restore the lost human ability to communicate freely and directly with other species.

We honour those that come to us for help, not judging, condemning, or invalidating them for their mistakes or misunderstanding but honouring their desire for change and harmony.

We know that to keep this work as pure and harmonious as possible requires that we continually grow spiritually. We realize that telepathic communication can be clouded or overlaid by our own unfulfilled emotions, critical judgments, or lack of love for self and others. We walk in humility, willing to recognize and clear up our own errors in understanding others' communication (human and non-human alike).

We cultivate knowledge and understanding of the dynamics of human, non-human and inter-species behaviour and relationships to increase the good results of our work. We get whatever education and/or personal help we need to do our work effectively, with compassion, respect, joy and harmony.

We seek to draw out the best in everyone and increase understanding toward a mutually beneficial resolution of problems. We go only where we are asked to help, so that others are receptive and we truly can help. We respect the feelings and ideas of others and work for interspecies understanding, not pitting one side against another but walking with compassion for all. We acknowledge the things that we cannot change and continue where our work can be most effective.

We respect the privacy of people and animal companions with whom we work, and honour their desire for confidentiality.

While doing our best to help, we allow others their own dignity and help them to help their animal companions. We cultivate understanding and ability in others, rather than dependence on our ability. We offer people ways to be involved in understanding and growth with their fellow beings of other species.

We acknowledge our limitations, seeking help from other professionals as needed. It is not our job to name and treat diseases, and we refer people to veterinarians for diagnosis of physical illness. We may relay animals' ideas, feelings, pains, symptoms, as they describe them or as we feel or perceive them and this may be helpful to veterinary health professionals. We may also assist through handling of stresses, counselling and other gentle healing methods. We let clients decide for themselves how to work with healing their animal companions' distress, disease, or injury, given all the information available.

The goal of any consultation, lecture, workshop, or interspecies experience is more communication, balance, compassion, understanding and communion among all beings. We follow our heart, honouring the spirit and life of all beings as One.

www.petsofthehomeless.org

www.manataka.org

www.gypsymaggierose.com – Henry the pig

www.cell.com/current-biology/home – chimpanzee grief paper

www.save-me.org.uk – if you care about the plight of animals please join my friend, Brian May, in his quest here.

ANIMAL COMMUNICATORS

www.animaltalking.co.uk – Jackie Weaver

www.anexchangeoflove.com – Madeleine Walker

www.animaltranslations.com – Maureen Harmonay

healinganimals.org – Elizabeth Whiter

animalthoughts.com – Pea Horsley

centaur-therapies.co.uk – Holly Davies

www.animalscantalk2me.com – Oephebia

www.talkingwithanimals.co.uk – Linda Lowey

carolschultz.com – Carol Schultz

www.ukanimalhealer.co.uk – Niki Senior

www.simonfirthseminars.com – Simon Firth – Love Your

Life!

www.margretbarker.co.uk – this organization aims to:

- raise awareness of the contribution animals made in the wars of human conflict

- promote the spread of the Margaret Barker Memorial Wreath for Animals

- recognize the bravery taken and the sacrifice made by animals in wartime

- honour the companionship between man and animal, who worked, fought and died together in times of conflict

- give credence to and an enduring remembrance for their contribution.

Here are some links to videos that you'll enjoy and that may astound you:

www.youtube.com/watch?v=DgiyhKN_35g&feature=related – dog on motorway

www.youtube.com/watch?v=LU8DDYz68kM – baby water buffalo and lions

www.youtube.com/watch?v=cBtFTF2ii7U – elephant and dog

www.youtube.com/watch?v=d30RUgAZz1E&feature=channel – dog and lion

www.youtube.com/watch?v=orFHJVaSlUE&feature=related – monkey and kitten

www.youtube.com/watch?v=LAFHxgbybVw&feature=related – pig and tiger cubs

www.youtube.com/watch?v=9YO3aXwDr00 – cat CPR

www.wired.com/wiredscience/2010/04/chimpanzee-grief

news.nationalgeographic.com/news/2005/01/0104_050104_tsunami_animals_2.html – tsunami report on animals.

Hay House Titles of Related Interest

The Amazing Power of Animals, by Gordon Smith

The Animal Healer, by Elizabeth Whiter

Animals and the Afterlife, by Kim Sheridan

Communication with All Life, by Joan Ranquet

Pets Have Souls Too, by Jenny Smedley

ABOUT THE AUTHOR

Based in the beautiful county of Somerset, in the UK, and happily married for 41 years, **Jenny Smedley,** DPLT, is a qualified past-life regres—sionist, author, TV and radio presenter and guest, international columnist and spiritual consultant, specializing in the subjects of past lives and angels. She's also an animal intuitive and tree com—municator. She lives with her husband Tony, a spiritual healer, and her reincarnated 'Springador' dog, KC.

Her own current life was turned around by a vision from her one of her past lives, in which she knew the man known today as Garth Brooks. Problems and issues related to that life were healed and resolved in a few seconds. For two years she hosted her own spiritual chat show on Taunton TV, interviewing people such as David Icke, Reg Presley, Uri Geller and Diana Cooper. Jenny has appeared on many TV shows in the UK, USA, Ireland and Australia, including *The Big Breakfast, Kelly, Open House, The Heaven and Earth Show, Kilroy and Jane Goldman Investigates,* as well as featuring in hundreds of radio programmes, including *The Steve Wright Show* on BBC Radio 2, and *The Richard Bacon Show* on BBC Five Live, as well as in the USA, the Caribbean, Australia, New Zealand, Tasmania, Iceland, Spain and South Africa. She writes regular columns for five magazines in three countries.

Her most recent press appearances have been in:

The Daily Mail – 'World Renowned'
The Daily Express – 'Unique rapport with the natural world'
The Sunday Times Style Magazine – 'A global phenomenon'

She'd love to hear from you about your beloved pets, so please get in touch by emailing her at author@globalnet.co.uk and perhaps your pet will be immortalized in one of her future books.

www.jennysmedley.com